Celebrating

THE EASTER MYSTERY

Celebrating

THE EASTER MYSTERY

Worship resources for Easter to Pentecost

Edited by Christopher Irvine

MOWBRAY

Mowbray
A Cassell imprint
Wellington House
125 Strand
London, WC2R 0BB

215 Park Avenue South
New York, NY 10003

First published 1996

British Library Cataloguing-in-Publication Data

A catalogue record for this book is available from the British Library.

ISBN 0–264–67394–8

Typeset by Falcon Oast Graphic Art

Printed and bound in Great Britain by Biddles Ltd, Guildford and King's Lynn

CONTENTS

*Liturgical resource material composed and compiled by Christopher Irvine.

FOREWORD

The last few years have seen a great revival in the Church of interest in liturgical matters that has cut across previous party lines. As part of this process a whole series of liturgical resource books has been published that has been intended to help parishes rediscover the Church's rich liturgical traditions.

The publication, in particular, of *Lent, Holy Week and Easter* (1984) as a companion volume to the ASB, has made widely available a whole range of ceremonies and liturgies in Anglican form that were once seen as the possession of only a privileged few. In my travels around the parishes of my diocese I have been impressed by the seriousness and care with which many priests and congregations have entered into this journey of rediscovery. Many people have found their liturgical and spiritual life immeasurably enriched by taking part in these traditional and profoundly moving ceremonies.

This has, of course, led to an increase in the workload for those involved in organizing and leading these services, as Alan Gyle points out in his article on church music in this collection of essays (p. 68ff):

> [as] often as not, Easter morn is greeted with a sigh of relief, the
> struggle of Lent and Holy week is over for another year, and
> things can go back to normal (p. 69).

The feeling of tiredness that can come after a busy Lent and Holy Week is one that is shared not just by musicians, but by parish clergy and those in the congregation who have walked with them the road to Golgotha and Easter Day. It seems no accident that the traditional name for Easter 1, Low Sunday, accurately reflects the number usually in the congregation on the Sunday after the great Paschal celebration!

This book is intended as a resource to help overcome this tiredness. The careful theological explorations and practical suggestions are intended to encourage and to help those who prepare worship to view the season with renewed confidence, and to present services that continue the celebration of Easter in new and fresh ways.

The book is a timely reminder of the importance of the season of Easter, the great fifty days during which the celebration of the Paschal mystery is continued and explored. From a theological exploration of Orthodox icons to suggestions for an Easter sequence, the authors encourage us to enter more profoundly into this high season of celebration and the richness of its message.

For Easter *is* a time of celebration, a time of singing and joy. It is a time when the shout of 'Alleluia' rings out again and again in praise and adoration. Christ is risen and the whole world is made new in his resurrection life! During this holy season the words of that great Easter shout of praise, the *Exultet*, should enter into our very souls and lift us up before our God and Father with voices raised in ever grateful thanks:

> Rejoice, heavenly powers. Sing choirs of Angels!
> Exult all creation around God's throne,
> Jesus Christ our King is risen.
> Sound the trumpet of salvation.
> Rejoice. O earth in shining splendour, radiant in the brightness
>   of your King.
> Christ has conquered! Glory fills you! Darkness vanishes for
>   ever.
> Rejoice O Mother Church Exult in glory!
> The risen Saviour shines upon you!
> Let this place resound with joy, echoing the mighty song of all
>   God's people!

I warmly commend this book to all those who are involved in preparing and leading worship, and indeed to everyone who seeks to deepen their life in our Risen Lord.

Richard Harries,
Bishop of Oxford
July 1995

CONTRIBUTORS

JOHN BAGGLEY
is Rector of Bicester and is the author of *Doors of Perception* (Mowbray, 1987).

ELAINE BARDWELL
has been teaching New Testament Greek and Patristics at St Stephen's House, Oxford.

LESLIE FRANCIS
is D. J. James Professor of Pastoral Theology and Mansel Jones Fellow at Trinity College, Camarthen and the University of Wales, Lampeter.

ALAN GYLE
is the Succentor and Dean's Vicar of St George's, Windsor, and a member of the PRAXIS Council.

GORDON JEANES
is Sub-warden of St Michael's Theological College, Llandaff, and lecturer in Liturgy and Church history at University College Cardiff.

CHRISTOPHER IRVINE
Vicar of Cowley St John, lectures in Liturgy, is the author of *Worship, Church and Society*, (Canterbury Press, 1993), and a member of the PRAXIS Council.

GRAHAM WOOLFENDEN
is Lecturer in Liturgy at Ripon College, Cuddesdon and is the Chairman of the Society for Liturgical Studies.

ACKNOWLEDGEMENTS

The psalms reproduced in this volume are taken from *Celebrating Common Prayer*, which adjusts the Psalms published in *The Book of Common Prayer of the Episcopal Church in the USA*. The author is indebted to Brother Tristam of the Society of St Francis for his advice and to Charles Mortimer Guilbert, Custodian of the *Standard Book of Common Prayer of the Episcopal Church in the USA*.

The Collect for Purity and the Easter Anthems are reproduced from *The Alternative Service Book 1980* and are used with permission from The Central Board of Finance of the Church of England.

The English translations of the *Benedictus* and the *Gloria in Excelsis* prepared by the English Language Liturgical Consultation (ELLC), 1988, are used with permission.

D. H. Lawrence's poem 'The Phoenix' is reproduced with permission from Laurence Pollinger Ltd, and the estate of Frieda Lawrence Ravagli.

The Easter morning rite included in this volume was developed from an outline sketched by the late Brother Gilbert Sinden, a member of the Australian Province of the Society of the Sacred Mission.

Thanks are also due to Fr George Guiver of the Community of the Resurrection for his helpful comments on some of the liturgical texts.

Finally, thanks are due for the encouragement and professional assistance of Judith Longman of Mowbray, who was indispensable in bringing the project to completion.

Christopher Irvine
Oxford, 1995

INTRODUCTION

The aim of this book is to draw attention to the high season of the Christian year and to deepen Christian prayer and worship during the great Fifty Days from the Easter Vigil to the feast of Pentecost. This season is a time for festivity, a time of uninterrupted song, and is described by some of the earliest Christian writers in the most striking terms. Flushed with God's undying love Christians are given the space to rejoice and delight in creation's birthday. However this is not a cancelling of the cross, or a denial of human tragedy and sin, but an affirmation of Christ's victory over sin and death, the very ground of Christian hope. For although the mood of the Easter season is celebratory, it retains and affirms the conviction that the Risen Christ bears on his body the marks of suffering humanity, and Christians are ennerved and enabled by the Holy Spirit to engage those things which spoil creation and deprive human beings of their God-given dignity. The Easter season with its focus upon the death and vindication of Jesus and the gift of the Holy Spirit is the time *par excellence* for the enlivening of Christian witness. This book seeks not only to plug a gap, but to enrich Christian celebration of the Easter season, and was conceived on the basis that such celebration is the most immediate source and inspiration of Christian life. So, in the widest sense of the term the book is offered as a resource book.

Celebrating the Easter Mystery consists of essays and liturgical texts which draw insights from a wide ecumenical spectrum, and it recovers patterns of prayer from the deep streams of Christian worship. The essays are intended to widen the reader's appreciation of the riches of Christian celebration during the Easter season. Each has a direct practical bearing on how Christians may celebrate and be touched and transformed by the Easter mystery of Christ's death and resurrection. The liturgical texts and suggestions for worship, preaching and prayer in the context of the home have been inspired by a wide variety of liturgical traditions, including domestic Jewish practice, the writings of the seventeenth-century Anglican liturgist Jeremy Taylor, texts and the practice of Eastern traditions; the exercise has not been one of liturgical archaeology, but an attempt to capture the vibrancy of this season in forms which echo Scripture and tradition and speak to the contemporary Christian imagination. Each item in this book should resonate with the depths of Christian tradition, engage with contemporary theological reflection on the meaning of Christ's death and resurrection, and offer to the whole Christian family of churches a resource book which should help to nurture resurrection faith. A faith which casts its light back upon the present, so that even those who presently stand in the shadow of the cross can see a new horizon and a way of being alive to God and committed to the world.

Christopher Irvine
Oxford, 1995

CELEBRATING THE EASTER VIGIL

Liturgically speaking the Easter Vigil celebrated on the night of Holy Saturday is the climax of the Christian year. It is the Christian Passover, the Christian Pasch, which holds together through word, symbol, and ritual enactment the whole saving work of Christ. As such it is a unitive celebration, not re-enacting any single historic episode, or aspect of the story of Jesus' passion, death and resurrection, but presenting it whole as God's work of saving his people. This unitive sense was perfectly caught by the ancient Christian word 'Pasch', which denoted both the passion of Christ, and his passing over, his *transitus*, from death to life. In early Christian writing the Pasch was often described in paradoxical language, and through this device Christian poets and preachers were able to combine the whole saving drama of God, from the Incarnation to the Ascension, in a single stanza. Thus, the second-century Melito of Sardis could say in a Paschal homily:

> It was he that was enfleshed in a virgin,
> that was hanged on a tree,
> that was buried in the earth,
> that was raised from the dead,
> that was taken up to the heights of the heavens.[1]

Like the poetry of the early Christian preacher, the ceremonies of the Easter Vigil fuse together all that is commemorated and celebrated throughout the whole Christian year, and present the saving work of God in a strikingly dramatic and arresting way. One might say that at the Easter Vigil the whole Christian story bears upon us, and through its symbols and sacramental signs makes present for us the saving reality of which it tells. Needless to say, such a rich and potent celebration demands that it is carefully and prayerfully prepared for. Exactly how it is to be celebrated will depend to a large measure on the resources of the worshipping community, and the architectural ordering of the building in which it is to be celebrated, and therefore what follows in this essay is not so much a step-by-step explanation of how the ceremonies might be celebrated, but an attempt to sketch out the basic shape of the service, to highlight its salient parts, and show how they relate to each other. It is crucial that those who preside at liturgical celebrations and have prominent roles to play as readers, singers and musicians, have some understanding of the under- lying shape of the liturgical rites and of how their words and gestures com- plement each other. The really important thing is for those words, symbols and actions to be sensitively handled and confidently declaimed in order that they might make their full impact upon the congregation. An understanding of the shape of a complex service like the Easter Vigil will certainly help to foster the necessary sensitivity and confidence required in those who have the privilege of leading the worship of the people of God.

The first task is to uncover the overall shape of the Vigil, and once that pat- tern has been established, to identify the component parts and see the sequence in which they might best be placed. It might be thought that the Easter Vigil is a kind of extended ministry of the Word, with the option of Communion being celebrated at the end, but its shape is basically fourfold. First, there is the Service of Light. Second, the Vigil proper with its Old Testament readings, psalms and collects. Third, the baptismal element; and fourth, the offering of the eucharist and Easter Communion. Structurally these four parts are inextricably linked and form an organic whole, and although the Vigil proper may precede the Service of Light, as suggested by the layout in *Lent, Holy Week, Easter*, these two component parts should not be dislocated, in the sense of choosing some parts and curtailing, or even omitting others. For as I hope to demonstrate, there is a kind of internal logic in the service. So let us examine each component part in turn and see how each relates to the others.

The Service of Light

The first point which needs to be clearly seen is that the Easter Vigil is a ser- vice for the night. The night of the Passover is essentially a time for watching (see Exodus 12:42) and the Easter Vigil shares this characteristic. Although it is a night service the watching of the Vigil need not be in total darkness; after all, the earliest Christians celebrated Christ's passover at the time of the full Passover moon, and furthermore, every evening, at Evening Prayer, Christians enter the darkness of the night with the radiant hope of the resur- rection.

So much then for those who say that a night service belongs to another and past age, and not to an age of artificial lighting. Services in the evening, espe- cially if candles are used, seem to be attractive and catch the popular imagi- nation. And in an inner-city area where the night time can be threatening and people are wary of walking the streets, the very act of kindling lights can be a reassuring and meaningful symbolic gesture.

The service of light in the Easter Vigil has its roots in the so-called lucer- narium, the ancient ceremony of lighting the lamps at the beginning of Vespers, or Evening Prayer. This ceremony was described by a number of early Christian writers, and most likely grew from the Jewish custom of lighting the Sabbath lamps on the eve of the Sabbath day. There are also possible precedents in the daily lighting of lamps in the temple at Jerusalem and in the classical custom of greeting the light in a pagan domestic setting. The lucernarium constitutes a central theological, as well as a ritual element of Evening Prayer. The kindling of a candle, or lamp, and the greeting of its light reminds us that Christians enter the darkness of the night with the light of the Risen Christ. The lucernarium persists in the Byzantine rite of Vespers, and has a long history in the Milanese rite in the West. The practice has been happily restored in a number of contemporary liturgical forms for Evening prayer, as provided for instance in *Celebrating Common Prayer*.

The lighting of the evening lamps, or candles, at Evening Prayer serves both a practical and a symbolic function. A service in the evening or at night requires some illumination, but there is also the symbolic function of the light which constitutes one of the key theological presuppositions of Christian prayer at the hour when the natural daylight fades and we enter the darkness of the night. Anglicans will be familiar with the classic evening collect: 'Lighten our darkness, we beseech thee, O Lord', which expresses one of the major themes of prayer at night. The symbolic gesture of lighting a candle at the beginning of Evening Prayer expresses well the conviction that we enter the darkness with the Risen Christ, the true light who never fades. And so it has become customary to open Evening Prayer with this symbolic demonstration of the truth of the resurrection, and to celebrate the presence of Christ, which neither darkness nor death can obscure or obliterate. This Vesper light is traditionally greeted with a song of praise, like the hymn 'O gladsome light, O grace', ascribed to the fourth-century bishop and prolific writer of hymns, Ambrose of Milan, or with some other form of praise prayer.

The present writer was recently privileged to take part in the celebration of Vespers on a Sunday in Milan Cathedral. The large cavernous church was in semi-darkness as dusk fell, and the ministers and servers entered with unlighted candles, but with one server bearing a lit oil-lamp. When the entrance procession reached the chancel step the two acolytes' large candles were lit from the lamp, and these in turn were used to light the candles on the altar. As these were being lit the chant praising the light was sung by the Officiant, and then the main electric lights of the building were switched on. The entrance in silence created a sense of expectation, and the gradual increase of light in the building helped to engender a celebratory mood. The gradual illumination of the whole building recalls the ancient practice in fourth-century Jerusalem, described by the pilgrim Egeria and recorded in her diary. According to her report every Saturday evening celebration in the church complex of the Anastasis and Martyrium had the same exuberance and dramatic impact as the Easter Vigil. Egeria's description of the actual Easter Vigil is tantalizingly brief, and concludes with the ambiguous comment: 'They keep their Paschal vigil like us.'[2]

However, in her description of a Vigil of the Resurrection, which apparently was celebrated each Saturday night, Egeria records the fact that a perpetual light burnt in the so-called Sepulchre, the cave where allegedly Jesus was buried. At this service the congregation gathered in the Anastasis, the church built by Helena, the Emperor Constantine's mother, which enclosed the Sepulchre, and the light was brought out from the cave and was then quickly passed from person to person as they lit their individual candles and tapers, which created, according to Egeria, 'a blaze of light'. Something like this was imported into the practice of churches in the West, and became a feature of the Easter Vigil. In Spain, for instance, the light was kindled secretly in the sacristy of the church, and then dramatically brought into the darkened church where it was greeted by the people with the triple acclamation: 'Lumen Christi' (the light of Christ), as the light spread around the whole congregation.

In some places in medieval England, such as York, Prudentius' hymn praising the light, 'Inventor rutuli', would be sung as the newly lit Paschal candle was processed through the nave of the church. (See Appendix A for a translation of Prudentius' hymn.)

In the splendid basilica of St John Lateran in Rome, two large·candles were used at the Easter Vigil. They were placed on either side of the pope during the readings, and were then taken in procession to the baptistry where they would serve to give light for the baptisms. After the celebration of baptism the two candles would lead the newly enlightened into the main body of the church, and would then be placed on the altar for the offering of the Eucharistic Prayer. So in Rome the light primarily served a utilitarian function, but this is not to say that its symbolic import was unregistered.

In Northern Italy, and in large areas of France, a special Easter candle came to be used at the Easter Vigil, and this soon became general practice in the Western Church. In general terms, what emerged as the point of difference between the 'evening light' kindled at Vespers, and the 'Easter light' greeted at the Easter Vigil, was that the former was praised and the latter was blessed; but there is clearly a family resemblance between the two ceremonies, and it is generally accepted that the service of light at the Vigil developed from the practice of the lucernarium at Vespers. The form of blessing for the Easter candle came to be known as the *Laus Cerei*, and the earliest extant blessings are ascribed to Ennodius, the sixth-century Bishop of Pavia. The words of these blessings indicate that the Easter candle was no ordinary taper, or tallow candle, but was a special and expensive candle made with beeswax, to mark the solemnity of the occasion. As all objects used for religious purposes, the Easter candle soon attracted a symbolic meaning, and came to represent a microcosm of the physical world penetrated by the brilliance of God's redemptive love in Christ.

The Hebrew Scriptures tell how God manifested himself to Moses in the burning bush (Exodus 3:2), and so the flame of the candle soon came to represent the appearing of Christ. The beeswax, the material substance of the candle, was believed in the classical world to be produced parthenogenetically, and so came in Christian rhetoric to symbolically represent Jesus' birth from a pure virgin. The wick, made from papyrus, was seen to represent the waters of the earth which it was believed Christ hallowed by entering the water of the River Jordan at his baptism. Thus the Easter candle, as a physical object, became a symbol of the natural world into which God manifested himself and entered in Christ. And Christ, according to the prologue of John's gospel, is the light who enlightens all people.

Such a complex symbolic reading was not universally approved of. The fourth-century saint and scholar Jerome in a letter to a deacon named Praesidius expressed his disapproval of the florid style of the deacon's prayer of blessing for the Easter candle, and the borrowing of images and rhetorical forms from classical literature. Nevertheless, the symbolic meanings associated with the Easter candle persisted, and this is clearly illustrated in the *Deus mundi conditur*,[3] a form of blessing for the Easter candle which appears in the eighth-century Gelasian Sacramentary, in which God is praised for the victory of light over darkness, and as in the writings of Virgil, the bees are praised for their industry, organization and extraordinary powers of procreation: 'Bees are economical and chaste in reproduction. They build cells with wax which even a master craftsman could not match.'

We can also infer from Jerome's letter that the task of blessing the Easter candle was assigned from earliest days to a deacon, and the persistence of this tradition is seen in some of the illustrated scrolls of the Paschal proclamation, such as the one from Beri, which shows a deacon blessing a large Easter candle, tapered finely at the top, and appearing to be at least five foot in height. The established custom was that once the Easter candle was kindled and placed in its prominent holder, the deacon would sing the *Praeconium Paschale*, the Easter song of praise, most commonly called the *Exultet*. The *Exultet*, which gradually came to replace other songs of blessing such as the one mentioned above from the Gelasian Sacramentary, opens with a declaration of cosmic praise: 'Now let the angelic heavenly choir exult; let joy pervade the unknown beings who surround God's throne', and then proceeds to praise God for Christ's victory. After the dialogue, which is familiar to us as the opening of the Eucharistic Prayer, the *Exultet* reads like a kind of Christian Haggadah, a story with repeated allusions to the Passover, which unfolds the mighty work of God's redemption.

Notice that so far there has been no mention of the new fire, which we have come to associate as a central feature of the Easter Vigil service. The sole purpose of the new fire at the Vigil is to kindle the Easter candle, and thereby to provide some illumination for the Vigil service. Originally in Rome, as in Jerusalem, light for the Vigil on Holy Saturday was derived from a 'reserved', or perpetually burning lamp, and the use of a fire was a fairly late development in the evolution of the service. Once adopted, the major significance of the fire rested in the fact it was a *new* fire. All the lights and lamps in church were extinguished on Good Friday in order to give some symbolic representation of the cosmic significance of Jesus' death on Calvary, when 'darkness was over the whole earth' (Mark 15:33). The making of new fire by striking a flint on the night of Holy Saturday gave ample scope for symbolic embellishment and allegorical interpretation. The spark flying from the flint could represent Christ rising from the stone tomb, and so on. At first, the fire was generally kindled in a convenient place, either in an alcove, or under an archway in the church, or adjoining ecclesiastical building.

At the cathedral at Lyon in France the custom was to kindle the new fire behind the high altar, but the general practice in churches was to light the new fire in a convenient doorway, or in a monastic cloister, in order to protect the flame from the natural elements, and to make the lighting of the Easter candle a safe procedure.

By the eleventh century the use of outdoor bonfires had become fairly widespread, and this popular practice is undoubtedly an example of the Christianization of the pagan practice common in northern Europe of lighting bonfires to beckon the warmth of spring. The more recent enthusiasm for the construction and use of a bonfire on the night of Holy Saturday has been encouraged by the directive in the 1970 *Missale Romanum* that a 'large fire' should be prepared. The use of a bonfire brings a number of practical difficulties, and quite candidly can be unsafe: there is the risk of vestments catching alight and serious injuries from burns. But from a liturgical point of view, the problem of a fire on the scale of an outdoor bonfire is that it rather detracts from, and diminishes the visible flame of the Easter candle, which after all is the primary symbol of the ceremonies.

The object of the new fire, then, is to kindle the Paschal candle and not to create a spectacle. The candle is the primary symbol, and when lit becomes a symbol of the Risen Christ, 'the pillar of fire', who leads his people, as God's people were led of old, from slavery to freedom, from darkness to light. The candle as a symbol of Christ is signified in the ceremonies which take place at the new fire. There a cross is traced, or preferably scored onto the unlit candle and five grains of incense may be inserted to mark the shape of the cross.

Regarding practicalities, I have found that a small portable barbecue provides a suitable receptacle for the new fire, and this can be conveniently set up under the arch of the principal entrance to the church. Weather permitting, the congregation could gather outside the church for the blessing of the fire and the lighting of the candle. Once lit, the candle is traditionally carried by a deacon and leads the people into the darkened church. After each of the three acclamations: 'The Light of Christ', the light can spread through the congregation as the people's individual candles are lit.

The Vigil

The scheme for the Easter Vigil service proposed by the Joint Liturgical Group in 1971, and later adopted by the Church of England's Liturgical Commission and included in *Lent, Holy Week, Easter* suggests that the Vigil proper, with its Old Testament readings, psalms and collects, might precede the Service of Light and the lighting of the Paschal candle. This order of events was successfully followed at Portsmouth Cathedral, where the building was beautifully reordered, with the architectural plan being shaped by the movement of the Paschal journey from darkness to light, enabling the people to move from where they first gather to hear their foundation charter (the Vigil readings), through the place of baptism into a space arranged for the celebration of the eucharist, the Paschal candle being lit after the Vigil readings. But the acknowledged problem with this arrangement is that some light is required for the readings in a darkened church. At Portsmouth the vigil part of the celebration is preceded by the blessing of the new fire. This might help to overcome a practical problem by producing some light, and help in creating the appropriate atmosphere for a community gathering to tell its stories, but the arrangement negates the point made above that the primary purpose of the new fire is to light the Easter candle. For the sake of symbolic coherence the lighting of the Easter candle should not be dislocated from the blessing of the new fire. Liturgical symbols ought to be clearly focused, and the arrangement at Portsmouth does rather blur the focus at this point.

It has been suggested in *Waiting for the Risen Christ*,[4] that the Vigil preceding the Service of Light heightens a sense of expectation and anticipation among the congregation, and although the arrangement is consistent with one strand of a richly diverse liturgical tradition, a theological question needs to be put: What exactly are the congregation expecting, and when does it occur? The resurrection of Christ is not an event which can be enacted and historically commemorated as some other events, such as Jesus' entry into Jerusalem on the first Palm Sunday, neither can it be strictly correlated with the occurrence of some natural phenomenon, such as the breaking of the dawn. Consequently it might be more helpful not to describe the Vigil as a time of expectant waiting, but a time for reading, for silent reflection and prayerful response to what God has done and continues to do in the darkness and hiddenness of the night.

Furthermore, and in support of the view that the Vigil should follow the Service of Light, the point can be made that what is read and listened to at the Vigil is heard and understood in the light of Risen Christ, for he, after all, is that light which 'shines in the darkness', and which was not overcome by the darkness, or held in the shadow of death. The Old Testament readings at the Vigil should not be regarded as 'prophecies', in the sense of looking to the future for their fulfilment, but narrative and poetic images which find their fullest meaning and vibrancy in relation to the Paschal Mystery of Christ.[5] For this reason, the readings are most appropriately read in the light of the Easter candle, which should be placed at the side of the lectern and reading desk. With this arrangement the lectern, which might be placed at the centre of the chancel step, is literally illumined by Easter light.

The congregation having extinguished their individual candles after the *Exultet*, the church is in semi-darkness for the duration of the readings. After all it is night, and we might also remember that Mary Magdala came to the tomb while it was still dark, and that the old words of the *Exultet* presupposed a night setting for the blessing of the Easter candle: 'May the morning star find the light still burning.'

For God's stupendous new act of re-creation, Christ's passover from death to life was unseen, unwitnessed, and belongs to the darkness of the night. The very poignancy of the night and its deep religious significance was superbly expressed by an important, though frequently overlooked figure of the twentieth-century Liturgical Movement, Aemiliana Lohr, a nun of Herstelle, who in a devotional commentary on the services of Holy Week wrote of the resurrection in these terms:

> This marvellous event belongs to the night. No other time saw
> it. Night embraces the beginnings of God's life in the world;
> into the night and the darkness of sin was this life born, to
> change all into light and day. In the night the child Jesus was
> born from the virgin's womb; in the night the man Jesus was
> born again from the womb of the grave.[6]

The night service of the Vigil is essentially a series of Old Testament readings, each with their own psalm and collect prayer. It is sometimes said that this part of the service is an anticlimax after the drama of the light ceremonies and the singing of the *Exultet*, and that people find the readings interminable and tedious. If this is the case, then efforts should be made to help people to maintain a proper level of prayerful attention during this part of the celebration. This would certainly be helped if the appropriate mood is set by those who are presiding over the celebration, and if the readings are declaimed well, unhurriedly, and at a measured pace. No fewer than four readings ought to be carefully selected, and after each reading there ought to be a sufficient pause to allow and encourage reflection and prayer. The readings are essentially food for reflection and the response to the readings takes the form of an appropriate psalm and a collect, which effectively gathers in a single voice the individual prayers of the whole assembly.

Of course, efforts could be made prior to the celebration to help those likely to attend the Vigil to appreciate the importance and function of this part of the celebration. An article could be written in the parish magazine addressing some of the attendant issues, or a Lenten Bible study could look at the various readings in turn. In all this the point which needs to be communicated is that the function of the Old Testament stories which are read and heard at the Vigil help to locate the congregation within the wider community of Israel, and to reinforce their identity as the people of God and the Body of Christ.

The service books include a wide selection of possible Old Testament readings. In the old Roman rite there were twelve readings, including the wonderful story from Daniel of Shadrach, Meshach, and Abednego in the fiery furnace. In Toledo Cathedral in Spain, the Vigil readings covered the full sweep of salvation history, but most selections fall under the general themes of creation, resurrection and baptism as the occasions when individuals are drawn into God's redeeming work in Christ. The new Roman rite offers seven readings:

1. The story of creation (Genesis 1).
2. The story of Abraham preparing to offer his son Isaac (Genesis 22).
3. The Exodus and the crossing of the Red Sea (Exodus 14).
4. The prophetic vision of the new Jerusalem (Isaiah 54).
5. The declaration of God's gracious offer of salvation (Isaiah 55).
6. The challenge to lay hold of wisdom (Baruch).
7. The promise of God's gift of a new heart and spirit (Ezekiel 36).

The Church of England's *Lent, Holy Week, Easter* offers a wider selection of twelve readings, including the story of the Fall, of Noah and the flood, Job's well-known 'Man born of a woman' passage, and Ezekiel's vision of the valley of dry bones. All these readings give substance to the Christian hope of resurrection, and some have immediate bearing on baptism and add further levels of meaning.

After the collect prayer of the final reading there should be a marked change in both the mood and the tempo of the celebration. For the liturgy moves directly into the eucharistic synaxis with the singing of the *Gloria in excelsis*. As a canticle the *Gloria* was first associated with Morning Prayer, and as a hymn concerned primarily with the figure of Christ, it is eminently suitable as a form for greeting the Risen Lord. At the celebration the *Gloria* might be introduced by a fanfare played on the organ, and at that moment all the lights in the church should be switched on, the candles lit, and bells rung to create a truly festive mood. The present writer fondly remembers the first Easter Vigil he presided at in St Mary's, Stoke Newington, when he discovered a large wooden football rattle which had been placed at the side of the President's chair, by a parishioner who had a keen sense of how to keep festival.

The baptismal liturgy

Following the familiar pattern of the eucharistic synaxis the collect for the day is sung immediately after the singing of the *Gloria*, and then the assembly sits for the New Testament reading from Paul's letter to the Romans, which prepares the way for the third facet of the Easter celebration, the liturgy of Christian initiation. In this reading (Romans 6:3–11), Paul tells how Christians participate in the Paschal Mystery of Christ's death and resurrection through baptism. After the reading of this passage the gospel reading might be heralded by the singing of an Alleluia chant. Traditionally the word 'Alleluia' is neither spoken nor sung during the season of Lent, and the singing of an 'Alleluia' at this juncture in the celebration can again mark the switch from a season of preparation and penitence to the Easter season of praise and joyful exuberance. The traditional triple Alleluia chant sung at this point by the President at the Easter Vigil is a stirring and dramatic melody, beginning on a low note and rising to the highest note on the final syllable of the last 'Alleluia'. It is as if the singing begins in the depths of the tomb and soars with the Risen Christ to fill all things with a crescendo of echoing praise. During the singing of the Alleluia the people's candles should be lit in readiness for the proclamation of the Easter gospel. A short homily, rather than a full sermon, should be given after the reading of the gospel.

The liturgy of initiation follows immediately after the homily. This facet of the celebration consists of the celebration of baptism, the renewal of baptismal vows, and confirmation. There is one strand of liturgical tradition which suggests that the Easter Vigil is the most appropriate time to celebrate Christian baptism. The third-century Church Order, the *Apostolic Tradition*, ascribed to Hippolytus of Rome, presents the Easter Vigil as the climax and culmination of a lengthy period of formation in which the catechumens, those preparing to enter Christian life and share its obligations and responsibilities, were prepared to be joined to Christ, and transferred from 'the kingdom of darkness to the kingdom of light'.

The very baptismal process might be seen as the counterpoint to Christ's passing over from death to life, and the rite ritually enacts that same movement. As Paul says in his letter to the Romans: 'Do you not know that all of us who have been baptized into Christ Jesus were baptized into his death? We were buried therefore with him by baptism into death so that as Christ was raised from the dead by the glory of the Father, we too might walk in newness of life' (Romans 6:4). Because of this close association between baptism and Christ's death and resurrection, the Easter Vigil with its primitive Paschal character is undoubtedly an auspicious occasion on which to celebrate baptism and welcome new Christians. Tertullian, a North African Christian, at the end of the second century deemed 'The Passover' as providing the day of most solemnity for baptism, for on that day 'was accomplished our Lord's passion, and into it we are baptized'.[7]

Once Christianity became legal in the fourth century, and Christians worshipped in basilicas, baptisms would be celebrated off-stage, as it were, in a baptistry. During the baptism the congregation would remain in the nave praying for the candidates. This is the origin of the litany which we find in the baptismal liturgy in the Roman Easter Vigil service. In terms of present practice, it would seem appropriate at this stage of the celebration for the whole congregation to process with the ministers, servers and candidates, and gather around the font. This of course presupposes that the font is located at the West end of the church, which to my mind is probably the best location, not least because it allows for some physical movement from the font to the focus of eucharistic celebration. Such movement ritually enacts that crucial model of baptism as *transitus*, a movement from one place to another, as the people of Israel crossed the River Jordan to enter the land of promise. A physical movement or procession helps to express this understanding of baptism as *transitus*, which complements the more familiar Paschal model discussed above.

A litany might well be sung as the people move informally from their seats in the nave to the font. I suggest informally because the significant movement is from the font to the eucharistic table. At the font the water should only be blessed if there are candidates to be baptized. The renewal of baptismal vows, a fairly recent addition having only been introduced into the Roman rite in 1951, is not without its problems. Strictly speaking, vows are not taken at baptism, and perhaps it would be more appropriate to describe this aspect of the rite as the renewal of the baptismal covenant. The nomenclature may be clumsy and theologically top heavy, but it might remove certain misunderstandings invited by the idea of renewing vows.

In *Lent, Holy Week, Easter* the form for the renewal of baptismal vows simply replicates the triple questions of the baptism service ('Do you turn to Christ? Do you repent of your sins? Do you renounce evil?') with the minimal triple credal questions with their rather bald response: 'I believe and trust in him.' Because of the brevity of these credal questions they unfortunately suggest a rather functionalist, and almost tritheistic presentation of the Trinity. It would be preferable if the candidates, together with the whole congregation, responded to the credal questions by reciting the appropriate sections of the Apostles' Creed, as is the general custom in most other Anglican baptismal liturgies. If candidates have been baptized, then the congregation may be sprinkled with the baptismal water from the font immediately after the affirmation of faith. The actual sprinkling of water ought to be a generous and expansive gesture, with the water literally being thrown over the people. As this is being done, the antiphon from the Roman rite may be sung, or some other suitable sentence from Scripture may be dramatically declaimed.

The offering of the eucharist and Easter Communion

The baptismal liturgy at the Easter Vigil should move directly into the eucharist, which is the principal Mass of the whole Christian year, and its celebration should not be postponed until a later time of the day. Ideally the Easter Vigil should begin at such a time during the night that the eucharist will be celebrated when the dawn is beginning to break. On this occasion the Peace, with its Easter 'Alleluias' in the greeting and the response, might be given at the font as a way of concluding the baptismal liturgy, and welcoming the newly baptized into the Body of Christ. It is, of course, the offering of the eucharist and the sharing of the holy gifts of Communion which constitutes the congregation as the Body of Christ, and this is the principal reason why the baptismal liturgy should unfold into the celebration of the eucharist.

If the Peace is offered and exchanged as the people are still around the font, then a procession can move through the nave of the church singing an appropriate hymn, such as 'Come, ye faithful raise the strain' (NEH 106), towards the eucharistic table , which would ritually enact that movement of God's people to the place of 'milk and honey'. It would be especially appropriate if the newly baptized carried and presented the gifts of bread and wine for the eucharist on this occasion. The procession to the altar bearing the bread and wine for the eucharist is a vivid reminder that Communion, in which Christians are sustained as Christ's Body, and nourished with his very being and life, is the culmination of Christian initiation, the point and purpose of the journey of faith.

Writing in the middle of the second century, Justin Martyr describes in his first *Apology* how the newly baptized were brought from the baptismal bath into the eucharistic assembly where they were duly greeted and took their place for the celebration of the eucharist. The eucharist and our Easter Communion is a special moment of encounter with the Risen Lord. In *Lent, Holy Week, Easter* a prayer is provided in a section for the blessing of an Easter garden which asks that we might meet Christ, but according to the Johannine Easter gospel (John 20:1–10), it is Christ who meets us, and calls us, as he called out 'Mary' in the garden on the first Easter morning. The point of the Easter Mystery so dramatically and comprehensively expressed in the Easter Vigil, is that the Risen Christ encounters us. It is not that we find him, or discover an empty tomb, but that he finds us, and makes himself known to us. The most intimate moment of that encounter is our Easter Communion.

After the Communion, it would seem fitting for the celebrations to continue in a more social and informal vein, perhaps with the congregation extending the feasting with a shared parish breakfast. After all, the Easter season was described as a *laetissimum spatium*, a broad space in which to make joyful festival.

> You who are first and you who are last, receive the same wage;
> you who are rich and you who are poor, dance together; you
> who are weak and you who are strong, celebrate this Day
> together; you who have kept the fast and you who have not,
> rejoice together today. The Lord's table has more than enough
> for all: enjoy his royal banquet. He has prepared the fatted calf:
> no one need go away hungry. He invites us all to enjoy the ban-
> quet of faith, to receive the riches of his goodness. None of us
> need grieve over his poverty, for Christ has revealed his univer-
> sal Kingdom and we are all members of it.[8]

NOTES

1 S. G. Hall, *Melito of Sardis* (Oxford: Clarendon Press, 1979), pp. 38–9.
2 J. Wilkinson, *Egeria's Travels to the Holy Land* (Warminster: Aris and Phillips, and

Jerusalem: Ariel Publishing House, 1981), p. 138.

3   See Appendix B for a translation of this text.

4   M. Perham and K. Stevenson, *Waiting for the Risen Christ* (London: SPCK, 1986), pp. 99 & 107.

5   For a fuller exposition of this view see C. Irvine, *Worship, Church and Society* (Norwich: Canterbury Press, 1993), ch. 5.

6   A. Lohr, *The Great Week* (London: Longmans, Green and Co Ltd, 1958), p. 146 (English translation).

7   E. C. Whitaker, *Documents of the Baptismal Liturgy* (London: SPCK, 1987), p. 9.

8   *The Paschal Homily* of St John Chrysostom, from an unpublished English translation by Gilbert Sinden SSM.

2

AN EASTER VIGIL HOMILY

This is the night

At the Jewish Passover it is the youngest son who asks the searching question: 'Why is this night so different from other nights?' In the *Exultet*, the Paschal proclamation, the expression '*This* is the night' is a frequent refrain, and like the Jewish child we too might ask: Why is this night so different? Our celebration tonight is different from the other celebrations and solemn observances of Holy Week: it stands apart with its peculiar vibrancy and resplendence. Our other celebrations this week have been driven by the imperative to remember, and have attempted to recreate and recapture the historical events and objective happenings of the last days and hours of our Lord's earthly ministry.

At the beginning of the week on Palm Sunday, the purpose of our procession, with its singing and mood of carnival, was to recreate our Lord's triumphant entry into the city of Jerusalem. On Maundy Thursday, our intention with the foot-washing was to recover something of the loving intimacy and apprehension which was felt and experienced by those gathered in the Upper Room. On Good Friday with the veneration of the cross, we were faced with the hard fact of the Lord's cruel death. But tonight, our celebration is different, for *this* is the night. We are not here, as we might gather for a performance of a passion play, or some other pious theatre, to reconstruct some past historical happening, for this is God's Passover; when the God of Israel, in raising his Son from the deep caverns of death, passes among us; passes through us, to be ahead of us and startle us into a surprising future. This is the night: *tonight*, the past, the present and the future are rolled into one. This is the night when God's salvation will dawn in us; not in time past, but here and now in this place, God the Father, in the power of the Spirit, seeks to draw us into the pattern of Christ's death and resurrection. And in him, the Alpha and the Omega, our individual pasts and our futures are held together and find their coherence and fulfilment.

At the calamity of Calvary, darkness fell on the earth, and day became as night; at this celebration our night is turning to day. Before the cross, before the unimaginable horror of the death of God, our words lost their currency, and our voices were silenced. Today a song is placed in our mouths, and the rich and resonant symbols of fire and water, bread and wine, are placed into our hands as the commerce of our salvation.

Tonight we are to realize that the type of Abraham's sacrifice of Isaac has been fulfilled. We have provided the wood and made the fire, and God has given the victim in his Son. So, our celebrations began with the blessing of the new fire. But unlike Moses who stood in awe before the burning bush, we ourselves are drawn into the fire; drawn by its flickering light to the centre of its heat, so that we might be purged of sin and purified, and feel the burning anguish of suffering humanity. We are drawn into the crucible of God's love, to arise, like the Phoenix, made new by Christ. It is dangerous to play with fire, but the fire of divine love is irresistible and dangerous. This much at least was seen by that English prophet of earthly passion, D. H. Lawrence, when he wrote that startling poem 'The Phoenix':

> Are you willing to be sponged out, erased, cancelled,
>   made nothing?
> Are you willing to be made nothing? dipped into oblivion?
> If not, you will never really change.
> The phoenix renews her youth
> only when she is burnt, burnt alive, burnt down
> to hot and flacculent flesh.
>
> Then the small stirring of a new small bub
> in the nest with strands of down like floating ash
> shows that she is renewing her youth like the eagle
>   – immortal bird.

Like the eagle. Tonight we have heard God say: 'You have seen what I did to the Egyptians, and how I bore you on eagles' wings and brought you to myself' (Exodus 19:4). In and with Christ we too have been borne up on eagles' wings, and this raising is more than a restoration of what has been lost. No, he has borne us on eagles' wings, raised us to even greater heights, even to the heavenly places; raised up as on the wings of the soaring eagle so that we might see with piercing clarity things old and new; that we might see our own lives in their true perspective and fearlessly envision a future.

In our celebrations tonight there is not only fire, but water, for we cannot face the light of God's new day unless we are born anew, through water and the Spirit. When a woman is about to give birth, the first thing to happen is the 'breaking of the waters', the rupturing and release of the amniotic fluid which had protected the foetus in the womb of its mother. In a few moments the baptismal waters will literally break upon us, vividly signalling our new birth into the light of God's new creation, and the glory of his kingdom.

Then, having been refreshed and revived by the baptismal waters, we will with open hearts and joyful expectation take our places at the Easter feast, surrounded by all God's angels and saints, and receive the blessed fruits of that redemption wrought for us by the Lamb who was slain, and now lives and reigns with the Father and the Holy Spirit, one God, for ever and ever. Alleluia. Amen.

3

PROCLAIMING THE RESURRECTION:
A RITE FOR EASTER MORNING

A rite for Easter morning for those churches which do not celebrate the Easter Vigil on the night of Holy Saturday. It is envisaged that this rite will be used before the celebration of Communion. The rite begins when people have assembled outside the door which is the usual entrance into the church. It is a dramatic rite commemorating how the disciples came to the tomb on the first Easter morning, and were there met by the Lord of life who had been raised gloriously from the dead. First the Easter Gospel is declaimed, his victory celebrated, and the people's response expressed in prayer for the Church and the wider world. Both the form and the content of the rite has been inspired by the Orthodox Easter ceremonies. In this rite the officiating minister represents Christ and knocks loudly and insistently upon the principal door of the church. At this point, the church building represents the cold stone tomb, and we recall that Christ comes to summon us to life as he called Lazarus from the dead.

The officiating minister and people gather before the main door of the church. The minister holds a large lighted candle; the people hold unlit tapers or candles. The minister greets the people:

> Christ is risen. Alleluia, alleluia!
> **He is risen indeed. Alleluia, alleluia!**

The minister continues:

> Dear friends, Christ has been raised gloriously from the dead, and the morning star has risen. Come and share the brilliance of his risen splendour, for he has called us out of darkness into his own marvellous light. May we all shine as lights in the world to the glory of the Father.

CELEBRATING THE EASTER MYSTERY

Each member of the congregation comes to the minister to light their individual taper, while the choir sing an appropriate hymn, such as 'Hail, Easter bright, in glory dight!' (NEH 108), or the Taizé chant: 'The Lord is my light, my life and salvation.' After all the candles are lit, an 'Alleluia' is sung to greet the Gospel, which is announced in the customary way.

The gospel: John, chapter 20, verses 1–9.

After the gospel the people respond:

> **Alleluia, allelulia, alleluia!**

Verses from Psalms 68 and 118 are then said or sung with the following response:

> **Christ is risen from the dead:**
> **By his death destroying death**
> **and raising those in the grave to life.**

1   Let God arise and let his enemies be scattered;
    let those who hate him flee before him.

> **Response.**

2   Let them vanish like smoke when the wind drives it away;
    as the wax melts at the fire,
    so let the wicked perish at the presence of God.

> **Response.**

3   But let the righteous be glad and rejoice before God;
    let them also be merry and joyful.

> **Response.**

4   The same stone which the builders rejected;
    has become the chief corner-stone.

> **Response.**

5   This is the Lord's doing;
    and it is marvellous in our eyes.

> **Response.**

6   On this day the Lord has acted;
    we will rejoice and be glad in it.

> **Response.**

The following Litany may be said, or sung:

In peace let us pray to the Lord;
Lord have mercy, Lord, have mercy, Lord, have mercy.

That our Saviour Jesus Christ may grant us victory over the powers of darkness, let us pray to the Lord.
Lord, have mercy.

That in the power of Christ's resurrection we may triumph over every temptation, and resist all deadly sin, let us pray to the Lord.
Lord, have mercy.

That we may know the raising up power of God, and be filled with the light and love of Christ, let us pray to the Lord.
Lord, have mercy.

That we may be radiant with the joy of Christ's resurrection, let us pray to the Lord.
Lord, have mercy.

That we may be summoned to share the wedding banquet of the Lamb, and rejoice with the whole company of heaven, let us pray to the Lord.
Lord, have mercy.

Grant to us, O Christ our God, so to live in the light of your resurrection that the radiance of your glory may be manifest and your saving help be known in all the world, for you are the Resurrection and the Life, and to you, your eternal Father, and to the all-holy good, and life-giving Spirit, we give glory for ever and ever.
Amen.

The minister, holding the lighted candle, approaches the main door of the church, knocks upon it and says the following verses from Psalm 24 with a loud voice:

> Lift up your heads, O gates;
> lift them high, O everlasting doors;
> and the King of Glory shall come in.

From inside the church, a voice replies:

> Who is this King of Glory?

The minister responds:

> The Lord, strong and mighty,
> the Lord mighty in battle.
>
> Lift up your heads, O gates;
> lift them high, O everlasting doors;
> and the King of Glory shall come in.

The voice again demands:

> Who is he, this King of Glory?

The minister declares:

> The Lord of hosts,
> he is the King of Glory.

At this point the doors are flung open, the minister strides in. The organ immediately strikes up with John of Damascus' hymn 'The day of resurrection' (NEH 117), and the people enter the building so that there is an inrush of light and praise.

The Communion resumes at the collect.

GRAHAM WOOLFENDEN

THE FIFTY DAYS OF PASCHA:
THE BYZANTINE TRADITION

A friend of the present writer is a cantor in his local Carpatho-Russian Catholic[1] parish church, and told of a visit to the church by a group of Roman Catholics one Eastertide. The thing that struck them most was the repeated singing of the Easter *troparion*.[2] As they said, whatever you believe beforehand, when you leave church you know one thing quite definitely: Christ is risen! In all the churches of the Byzantine liturgical tradition, Orthodox and Catholic,[3] the pre-eminence of Easter as the Feast of feasts is assured.

The services that cover Easter and its fifty-day extension to Pentecost are contained in the liturgical book called, appropriately, the *Pentecostarion*.[4] This book is one of those that contain the variable parts of the services, especially of Vespers[5] and Matins.[6] The eucharistic liturgy has a number of proper texts, especially on the greatest feasts, but on the whole, remains largely unchanged. The parts of the services that do not change are found in the *Horologion* or *Book of Hours*. The reading of the psalms in course is directly from the psalter; in other words, there is no single Breviary, or anything like a *Book of Common Prayer*, in which all the material may be found. As one might imagine, there is a vast amount of this liturgical poetry, originally scattered amongst many different collections. The codification process started around the eighth century, and the earliest collections for Lent and Easter date from the tenth century.[7] The separate *Pentecostaria* appear in the fourteenth century, the name first appearing in a manuscript of 1348.[8]

As has just been implied, the texts for Lent and Easter were at one time all in one collection, and so treated as a single cycle. The growing size of the repertoire of texts necessitated the division into separate books, and happening as this did well into the Middle Ages, the division had the effect of cutting off the ancient Easter Vigil from the rest of Eastertide. The last service in the *Triodion* is the Vespers and Liturgy of St Basil, now normally celebrated on Holy Saturday morning, which was the ancient Vigil of Pascha.[9] The first service given in the *Pentecostarion* is Matins of Easter Sunday morning, which normally starts at midnight,[10] and which is the service that most people identify as the Byzantine Easter celebration *par excellence*.

The Vigil Vespers and liturgy of St Basil

The original Paschal Vigil, with its lengthy series of readings and the baptism of those who had prepared for that event during Lent, eventually started with the light ceremony associated with Vespers, and a large number of other vesperal elements;[11] it also commenced at a reasonably suitable time for such a service, about four o'clock in the afternoon.[12] This might seem early for an Easter Vigil, but by this stage, the Vigil and earlier liturgy were followed, after a pause (which might include refreshment),[13] by Matins and the morning liturgy; the Vigil was very much an all-night affair! The service now celebrated on Holy Saturday morning is often drastically abbreviated. In Greece, and in churches that follow the Greek customs, this is the liturgy at which (or around which) most people make their Easter Communion.

The service begins with the opening psalm and litany of Vespers (the reading from the psalter is omitted); the clergy, in Slavonic use, are wearing dark vestments.[14] At the evening psalms (referred to by the opening words as 'Lord I have cried') the first *stichera* are from an ordinary Sunday in tone one, the others are proper and sing of the harrowing of hell: 'Today hell groans and cries aloud: "My power has been destroyed . . ."'[15] The struggle for life over death is not yet complete, but death and hell are staring defeat in the face.

The usual 'entrance' of Vespers and the singing of the ancient hymn 'Hail gladdening light' may be seen as a parallel to the light ceremony of the Western Easter Vigil. There now follow the Vigil readings, of which there are no fewer than fifteen. In a tenth-century Constantinople *Typicon*, the Patriarch went to the Great Baptistery after the first reading, and there were only fifteen if it took him that long to complete the baptisms.[16] The sixth reading is the account of Israel's crossing of the Red Sea, and the reading is continued by the singing of the canticle, 'The horse and rider he has thrown into the sea', with the choir responding 'For gloriously has he been glorified.'[17]

The Exodus reading is one that we associate with the baptismal nature of the feast of Easter, but some of the readings are more directly concerned with the resurrection.[18] The fourth is the account of Jonah's three days in the belly of the great fish, the eighth tells of Elijah raising the child of the Sidonian widow (I Kings 17:8–24), the tenth, Abraham's sacrifice of Isaac (Genesis 22:1–18). The fifteenth, the account of the saving of the three young men in the furnace, Shadrach, Meshach and Abednego, from Daniel 3, leads into the canticle *Benedicite* with its frequently repeated refrain 'Praise the Lord, sing and exalt him throughout all the ages!'[19] This story was also seen as foretelling Christ's three days in the tomb and his resurrection.

The *Benedicite* was immediately before the Patriarch entered the Great Church of the Holy Wisdom with the newly baptized. As they were anointed, the choir sang 'As many as have been baptized into Christ, have put on Christ. Alleluia!' (Galatians 3:27) as a response to Psalm 92: 'The Lord is King with majesty enrobed.' Then came the actual entry and the chant of Psalm 31:

'Happy the man whose offence is forgiven, whose sin is remitted.'[20] Today the singing of 'As many as have been baptized . . .' is done on all the ancient baptismal feasts; Easter, Pentecost, Christmas and Theophany (Epiphany), though without the psalms. It takes the place usually occupied by the Trisagion, 'Holy God, Holy Mighty, Holy Immortal have mercy on us.' The epistle reading that follows, from Romans 6:3–11 starts 'Do you not know that all of us who have been baptized into Christ Jesus were baptized into his death?'

We have now reached a moment of great drama; instead of the Alleluia chant, Psalm 82 is sung with the response, 'Arise, O God, judge the earth, for to thee belong all the nations.'[21] While this is being sung, the clergy change into their white, Paschal vestments, all dark hangings are removed from the church and replaced by bright ones,[22] and in Slav churches flowers, and Greek churches, green leaves, are scattered through the church and on the people. Now is read the resurrection gospel, Matthew 28:1–20, and the rest of the Liturgy of St Basil follows.[23] A striking feature of this day is the replacement of the Cherubic Hymn, at the entry of the gifts of bread and wine, by that from the old Jerusalem liturgy of St James, well known to English-speaking Christians as 'Let all mortal flesh keep silence.'

In earlier times, the liturgy finished at about 8 p.m., and those present received some blessed bread and wine, together with six dates or figs, and remained in church taking turns to read the Acts of the Apostles until about 11.30. The bread and wine are still blessed and distributed, and people take it in turns to read, but they do not all remain in church.[24]

The Midnight Services

The Midnight office is begun at about 11.30 p.m., and includes the reading or singing of the Holy Saturday Matins Canon 'Of old thou didst bury the pursuing tyrant beneath the waves of the sea. Now the children of those who were saved bury Thee beneath the earth.'[25] During the ninth ode of the canon, in the Slav usage, the clergy cense the Epitaphios (the embroidered representation of Christ lying in the tomb) which has lain in the centre of the church since Good Friday. It is then taken into the sanctuary and placed upon the altar, where it will remain until the eve of the Ascension.[26]

At midnight the Holy Doors of the Icon screen are opened and the clergy come out, vested in bright vestments and carrying lighted candles, to begin the Easter procession. In Greek churches this is preceded by a ceremony not found in the official liturgical books: the church is plunged into darkness at the end of the Midnight office, leaving only the eternal Vigil light behind the altar. The priest lights a candle from this, and comes to the doors (sometimes still closed, but the curtain open) singing: 'Come ye and receive light from the unwaning light; and glorify Christ, who has risen from the dead.'[27] This is then sung twice more by the cantors and the people's candles are lit: this can be highly dramatic, perhaps with the light passed by the priest over the doors to a cluster of waiting candles; in seconds there is a lighted candle in every hand, and the doors are opened for the procession. (This imitates the ceremony of the new fire in Jerusalem; it can be seen as representing light coming forth from the tomb of Christ.)

The procession customarily goes round the outside of the church, all take part, and only the sacristan should remain in church, lighting candles and filling the whole church with the smoke of incense. In Greek use the resurrection gospel of Mark 16:1–8 is read before the doors of the church, and the clergy sing the Easter *troparion* for the first time as bells are rung (and sometimes fireworks are let off!): 'Christ is risen from the dead, trampling down death by death, and upon those in the tombs bestowing life.'[28] In Slav use the celebrant holds a three-branched candlestick in his left hand, and sings the opening blessing before the closed doors of the church, after incensing them; then the *troparion* is begun. Verses of Psalm 67, 'Let God arise, let his enemies be scattered; let those that hate him flee before his face' are sung with the *troparion* as a refrain, the doors are flung open and all enter the well-lit church singing the hymn, and replying to the celebrant's cry of 'Christ is Risen!' with 'He is risen indeed!'

Most Western Christians associate Evening and Morning Prayer with the singing or saying of the psalms; by contrast, the only psalms sung at Byzantine Easter Matins are Psalms 67 (68) and 117 (118), and only a selection of the verses at that! The greater part of the service is made up of ecclesiastical poetry.[29] A *typicon* believed to date from 1122[30] also provides a Matins that lacks the specifically nocturnal element of long psalmody, and from the morning part of the office, Psalm 50 (51), which usually marks the change from the nocturnal part to the matutinal, and the Great Doxology.[31] Until recently, Easter Matins of the Roman rite was much shorter at Easter; all this was probably due to the Vigil taking up the time usually allotted to the nocturnal part of the morning office, so that was abbreviated.

After entering church, there is the normal Litany that comes at the beginning of most services: 'In peace let us pray to the Lord', and then the Paschal Canon. The canon, replacing the nine scriptural canticles once sung at this point, is an entirely poetic composition. There were patristic readings after the third and sixth odes (the second is normally omitted from poetic canons); and that found in several manuscripts as following the third ode, 'The day of resurrection' by Gregory Nazianzen, gives us the first words of the canon, well known to many English speakers from the hymn 'The day of resurrection! Earth, tell it out abroad.'[32] This is a quite faithful rendering of the first ode (comprising the *irmos* or theme song, and two *troparia* – *irmosy* usually contain a reference to the scriptural canticle, in this case Exodus 15) by John Mason Neale. Neale in fact set the whole canon to metrical verse, the following being his version of the *irmos* of the fourth ode, which draws its imagery from the canticle of Habakkuk 3:2–19, 'O Lord, I have heard the report of thee . . . God came forth from Teman, and the Holy One from Mount Paran':

Stand on thy watch-tower, Habbakkuk the seer,
And show the angel, radiant in his light:
'To-day,' said he, 'Salvation shall appear,
Because the Lord has ris'n, as God of Might.'[33]

At the beginning of each ode of the canon, the priests take it in turns to incense the altar, and then the people, greeting them: 'Christ is risen!', and after each ode, there is normally a short litany. The atmosphere of sheer joyful abandon is increased by the repeating of the *irmos* (often to a different melody) as a *katavasia*,[34] with the Easter *troparion* sung quickly three times. There are brief respites; after the third ode comes the *hypacoe* 'When they who were with Mary came, anticipating the dawn.'[35] A reading is required here but is not usually done. After the sixth ode is the *kontakion*, 'Though thou didst descend into the grave, O Immortal One, yet didst thou destroy the power of Hades'[36] and the *oikos* 'The myrrh-bearing maidens anticipating the dawn', itself followed by the hymn 'Let us who have beheld Christ's resurrection worship our holy Lord Jesus . . .'[37] The singing of the *Magnificat* before the ninth ode is replaced by 'Magnify, O my soul, Him who suffered willingly, and was buried, and arose from the grave on the third day'[38] which is followed by 'Shine, shine, O new Jerusalem, for the glory of the Lord has arisen upon thee; dance now and be glad, O Sion, and do thou exult, O pure Mother of God, in the resurrection of thy Son.'[39]

Another moment of calm is reached at the *exaposteilarion*, 'When thou hadst fallen asleep in the tomb as one mortal, O King and Lord, thou didst rise again on the third day, raising up Adam from corruption, and abolishing death; O Pascha of incorruption! O Salvation of the world!'[40] Many of the settings of this hymn, such as a well-known one by the late eighteenth-century composer at the Russian court, D.S. Bortnyansky, could be described as meditative or reflective: we are faced with a great mystery as much as we are celebrating a moment of great joy. The rejoicing is renewed with the 'Praises', verses from Psalms 148–50, and more *stichera*, then the Paschal verses with some of Psalm 67 (68) again, and lastly from Psalm 117 (118): 'This is the day which the Lord has made; let us rejoice and be glad in it' (a verse common to Eastern and Western Easter services); and the last verse: 'It is the day of resurrection; let us be radiant for the festival, and let us embrace one another. Let us say, O brethren, even to those who hate us: Let us forgive all things on the resurrection; and thus let us cry: Christ is risen from the dead . . .'[41] We not only sing of offering a fraternal kiss, we do so! The priest stands with the gospel book before the Holy Doors,[42] and all come up to kiss the gospels, to be greeted with 'Christ is risen!' and exchange the Easter kiss with the clergy and then with each other, three times, saying 'Christ is risen! he is risen indeed!'

One reading that does find a place at this service is the Easter Catechetical Homily attributed to St John Chrysostom. This sermon invites to the Paschal celebration both those who have faithfully kept the fast, and those who have not, for hell has been cheated of its prey. This sermon is, of course, well known to people, and it is customary for Greeks to repeat some of the words after the priest. First hell is characterized as 'embittered' and the people cry out 'Embittered' seven times; the reason for this bitterness is because 'Risen is Christ', also repeated several times as the words occur in the sermon.[43]

The night celebration continues with the liturgy; in some places, the Paschal Hour, which replaces Prime, Terce, Sext and None, is sung first.[44] The Liturgy of St John Chrysostom is used now, and has special antiphons at the beginning, while 'As many as have been baptized into Christ . . .' is sung instead of 'Holy God', as at the Vigil Liturgy. The epistle is Acts 1:1–8, in which the Risen Jesus promises the Spirit to his disciples; the gospel, John 1:1–17, is the prologue of John's gospel, and so both readings are new beginnings. This liturgy has a feeling of serene joy to it, but it must be admitted that in many places, most people do not wait for it, but go straight home to eat the soup of lamb entrails that was traditionally the first meat dish after the Great Fast.[45] Many try to get back home with the candles they have been holding still alight; then they can light their lamps before the icons, trace a cross over the door with the candle smoke, and perhaps, in rural areas, go out to the animals with the candle and sing the Easter *troparion* to them as well![46]

Food is a vital part of the Easter celebrations. A feast after the Easter Liturgy is normal, and there are special blessings for the meat and dairy products that many have abstained from during Lent. Various kinds of sausages, and other cooked meats, cheeses, eggs (dyed red), and much butter and milk, can all be found at the Easter table. Many bring their Easter baskets of food to church for them to be blessed. Besides savouries, sweets and cakes are provided in abundance, the Russian cake *kulich*, and the extremely rich cream cheese sweet *paskha*, are characteristic delicacies. If one has tried to keep the fast, then this feast makes the Paschal celebration an integral part of our lives in a very special way.

Renewal or Bright Week

Following the ancient tradition of beginning the liturgical day at sunset, one could say that the rest of Renewal Week (as Easter week is often known) begins with Vespers on Easter Sunday night. In Greek churches, this festal celebration is often referred to as the 'Vespers of Love', and in some places may be marked by a common celebration by the parishes of an area in a single large parish church or cathedral.

The service begins with the singing of the *troparion* and 'Let God arise', as do all main services this week. The opening Psalm 103 (104) and the reading of the psalter in course are omitted throughout the week. On 'Lord I have cried' are sung the same *stichera* as one would sing on an ordinary Sunday of the second tone; on Monday night will be sung those of the third tone, and so on (omitting the seventh tone).[47] It will be recalled that the resurrection hymns for the first tone were employed at the Saturday vesperal liturgy (see above), thus Bright Week is virtually a 'week of Sundays'.[48]

After 'Hail gladdening light', there is the Great *Prokeimenon*, 'What God is as great as our God? Thou art God who alone workest wonders.'[49] These much longer texts than usual, proper to each day of Bright Week, are relics of the older 'sung office' of *Hagia Sofia*[50] that have survived the fusion of that office with one that originated amongst Palestinian monks.[51] Now follows a reading from the gospel, John 20:19–25, relating Jesus' appearance to his disciples and breathing on them the Holy Spirit, but also recalling the doubts of Thomas, called the Twin. It is a Greek tradition for this gospel to be read in several languages; one book provides Greek, English, Latin, French, and German,[52] another has Slavonic, Serb, Romanian, Albanian, Arabic, Turkish, Armenian, Latin, Italian, English, Korean and Swahili, each provided with phonetic translation into Greek![53] Slav custom is to read the gospel at the Easter Sunday Liturgy in several languages, and in Ukrainian churches a bell is often rung between each section of the reading.

After the two normal litanies, the first of the *stichera* called *aposticha* from the resurrection service is sung, followed every day by the Paschal verses first sung at the end of Matins – this brings this festal Vespers to its end. During the rest of the week, Vespers is much the same but with no gospel reading. Matins is, throughout the week, largely a reprise of that sung at Easter Midnight, except that the Paschal verses are preceded by the resurrection *stichera* on the praise psalms (148–50), by each tone in turn as described above. Similarly, the daily liturgy in this week is the Easter Liturgy, which should conclude with the Easter procession as well. Where a daily liturgy is not possible, Easter Monday at least is observed as an important feast day.

The Renewal Week liturgies have their own epistles and gospels. The epistles begin a semi-continuous reading of the Acts of the Apostles that continues throughout the Paschal season. Those of this first week relate the choice of Matthias to replace Judas (1:12–17; 21–6), the event of the first Pentecost (2:14–21), Peter's Pentecost sermon on the resurrection (2:22–36), the account of the early community of the Church (2:38–43), the healing of a cripple by Peter and John (3:1–8), and Peter's declaration that this is a sign of the outpouring of God's power through the Risen Jesus (3:11–16). The tradition of reading Acts as the account of the results of the resurrection faith of the apostles, is nearest to the Easter experience itself in this week, as is only appropriate.

The gospels of Bright Week are mostly from John, taking it up from after the prologue read on Easter Sunday to include John's baptism of Jesus (1:18–28), the call of the first disciples (1:35–41), the dialogue with Nicodemus about the new birth (3:1–5), the cleansing of the temple (2:12–22), and John's foretelling his eclipse by Jesus (3:22–33); the exception is on Easter Tuesday, when Luke 24:12–35 (the road to Emmaus) is read. One can well understand these readings as addressed to the newly baptized, telling them what they are called to be as new born in Christ, devoted to God, and called to point beyond themselves to Jesus Christ by the quality of the lives

27

they live. The Lukan reading may well have been included as a eucharistic reference, since baptism, Chrismation[54] and Communion belong together. These readings also function as a reminder of the calling of all those baptized in Christ who have put on Christ; as we again sing throughout the week.

Beside the Easter service, the Friday of Bright Week has a commemoration of Mary, the Mother of God of the Life-Giving Spring. This service is described in the *Pentecostarion* as having no official place in the *typikon*, but placed here 'out of love for the Most Holy Theotokos'.[55] The readings, which strictly are additional to the Easter week ones, are the Christological hymn from Philippians (2:5–11), and Mary's choice of the 'good portion' (i.e., listening to Jesus rather than helping in the kitchen) in Luke 10:38–42 (also 11:27–8). These are standard readings for Marian feasts, the proper hymns take up the Easter theme of water in a new way: 'Thou dost ever gush forth streams of healings, O holy Virgin, unto them that come with faith to thy spring, O Bride of God . . .'[56] This imagery may well have been inspired by the Bright Friday reading from Acts about Peter and John healing a lame man, while 'Thy temple, o modest one, hath proved to be a supernatural place of healing for all, O Maid . . .'[57] may be distantly inspired by Jesus' cleansing of the temple, related in the day's gospel.

The imagery of water remains intimately connected with the whole of the Easter season, not least in this Week of Renewal. The repeated singing of the glorious Easter canon all week includes the words: 'Come, let us drink a new drink, not one marvellously brought forth from a barren rock, but the Source of incorruption, which springeth forth from the grave of Christ, in Whom we are established.'[58]

The Paschal season

The beginning of the reading of the Acts of the Apostles has already been noted. This is, however, not just the beginning of the Easter cycle of readings but of the semi-continuous cycle of reading that runs through the rest of the church year. From the Tuesday after Pentecost, Paul's epistle to the Romans is read, and a great part of the rest of the New Testament is then read, book by book, until the epistles of James, Peter, John and Jude are read in the pre-Lenten weeks.[59] The same is true of the gospels which are, with very few exceptions, read through entirely in the course of the year.[60] Very roughly, John is read through the Paschal season, followed by Matthew, much of Mark and Luke, and then the rest of Mark in the pre-Lent period and in Lent itself.[61] This lectionary system appears to have been in use since at least the eighth century.[62]

One of the results of this is that the great Johannine baptismal readings associated with Lent in the modern Roman rite (e.g. the Samaritan Woman and the man born blind) are Paschaltide readings in the Byzantine tradition. The Lenten Sunday readings, originally addressed to the catechumens, told them that they would see yet greater things (John 1:50), called for faith (like that of the paralytic in Mark 2:1–12), and for the taking up of the cross (Mark 8:34), as they begin to contemplate the death that Christ's life is leading towards (Mark 9:17– 31); a death, however, open to the hope of resurrection (Mark 10:34).[63] Many of the Paschaltide readings in the Byzantine tradition are intended to recall the baptism that has been administered.

The second Sunday of Easter, *Antipascha*, also called the Sunday of St Thomas, celebrates the faith which Thomas discovered (John 20:1–31): 'Thomas, touch my side with thy hand, saith Christ, and come, feel the print of the nails. Examine them in faith . . .'[64] and we pray that we may know the Risen Christ's presence now: 'Even as thou camest in the midst of thy disciples, O Saviour, and gavest them peace, come also amongst us and save us.'[65] During that following week, on Tuesday, is a commemoration of the departed known as *Radonitsa* in Slavonic. People visit the graves of their departed, and leave some Easter food on the graves. This purely Slav observance, of probably pagan origin, has no proper place in the liturgical books, but is a useful reminder in the season of resurrection of our hope for our departed.

The next Sunday, the Sunday of the Myrrh-Bearing Women, continues the resurrection theme with the account (from Mark 15:43–16:8) of the women's discovery of the empty tomb; an event remembered at every Sunday Matins in the verses known as the *Evlogitaria*. The poetry is often a dialogue: 'Why do you cry? Christ is risen!' 'Behold the grave and understand; for the Saviour is risen from the tomb.'[66] The following Sunday, of the paralytic man who lay beside the pool at the sheep-gate (John 5:1–15), returns us to the baptismal theme: 'Of old an Angel came down to the Sheep's Pool and healed one man every year; but now Christ doth cleanse endless multitudes by divine Baptism.'[67] The reflection is now on the effects of baptism in our lives; the first effect is healing; the next Sunday, that of the Samaritan woman (John 4:5–42), continues that healing and stresses the refreshing and life-giving powers of water. This Sunday is preceded on the Wednesday by the feast of Mid-Pentecost. The Vespers that commences this observance has three Old Testament readings; the middle one (a centonized reading of Isaiah 55 and 12) contains such references to water as ' . . . everyone who thirsts, come to the waters!' The gospel (John 7:14–30) is Jesus' challenging sermon at 'the middle of the feast', i.e. the Jewish Pentecost period. The texts stress the fruitfulness of the Risen Christ: 'Thou art an ever-flowing stream of true life, O Lord . . .'[68]

Jesus' words in the temple went on to call people to him to drink of life (John 7:37–9); here meet the themes of the living water, our reflection on what baptism has made us, and of the pouring out of the Spirit which we are looking forward to; the *troparion* of the day expresses it well: 'At Mid-feast give Thou my thirsty soul to drink of the waters of piety . . .'[69] All this is an allusion to the conversation of Jesus and this Samaritan woman on the true worship of God.[70] A further concrete expression of the symbolism of life-giving water is found in the *typicon*'s requirement that there be Lesser Blessing of

Water and then the Blessing of the Fields on this day. The Lesser Blessing is done at other times but is particularly well suited to this day, as yet another emphasis on the life-giving power of God poured out on every aspect of our lives.[71]

The final Sunday before Ascension is that of the man born blind (John 9:1–38), and functions as a reminder that the power of the Risen Christ is given to heal us, and make us able to see the truth and proclaim it: 'When Thou didst give eyes unto the man who had been blind from the womb, Thou didst say: Go, wash and receive thy sight, and glorify my Divinity.'[72]

Ascension is nearly upon us, but there is first the *apodosis* or conclusion of Easter, also known as the Leave-Taking. Most major feasts have their *apodosis* a week after the feast, Easter, as the Feast of feasts, has it forty days later! According to the Russian *typicon*, this day is celebrated just like Easter, the lovely hymns are repeated for the last time, the repeated singing of the Easter *troparion* and the Easter greeting are now given up, and at the end of the Liturgy, the *Epitaphios* is removed from the altar whereon it has lain since Easter night, back to its normal place.

The ceremonies of the Leave-Taking may put Western Christians in mind of the days when the Ascension marked a greater divide in Eastertide than it does now; a division that was dramatically marked by the extinguishing of the Paschal candle after the Ascension Day gospel. It should not be thought that Eastertide is now over for Byzantine Christians, as it tended to be in the past for Westerners. Ascension is a hinge point however, and the Leave-Taking ceremonies show that we are now moving into the second part of the Pentecost – the Fifty Days, a part more concerned with the gift of the Spirit.

Ascension itself is as one might expect. At Vespers, the Old Testament readings stress the ascent of the mountain of the Lord (Isaiah 2:2–3), the making ready for the return of exiles (Isaiah 62–3), and the Lord's kingship (Zechariah 14). The first *sticheron* on 'Lord I have cried' reminds us that Christ must go to the Father so that the Spirit may come: 'The Lord was taken up into the Heavens that He might send the Comforter to the world.'[73] This theme is repeated all the time, and at Matins, Mark's gospel is ended, whilst at the Liturgy, the epistle (Acts 1:1–12) and the gospel (Luke 24:36–53) are the normal Ascension readings. Now, and on the days that follow, the *troparion* is: 'Thou hast ascended in glory, O Christ our God, and gladdened Thy disciples with the promise of the Holy Spirit; and they were assured by the blessing that Thou art the Son of God and Redeemer of the world.'[74]

The Sunday between Ascension and Pentecost is known as the Sunday of the Holy Fathers, referring to those who assembled at the First Ecumenical Council at Nicaea in 325. The vesperal readings relate the blessings of Abraham by Melchizedech (Genesis 14), God's gift of the land and the power to judge (Deuteronomy 1), and the choice of the people of Israel to serve God (Deuteronomy 10). These readings are about faith and faithfulness, and the rewards that they bring. Nicaea met to deal with the Arian crisis and was the first of the many efforts that have been made, and must always be made, to unite all Christ's people into one as he prayed (the gospel of this Sunday, John 17:1–13): 'Truly comely are the feet of them that proclaim Thee, the Peace that passeth all understanding of all angels and men, O Christ, Who by the abundance of peace hast united the world.'[75]

The intervening Sunday is the Church struggling for the power to be what it must be, that power is in the outpouring of the Holy Spirit which we celebrate at Pentecost. Pentecost in the Byzantine tradition is also called Trinity Sunday, for it is the revelation of the nature of God as a Trinity of three Persons in one God. The Spirit is granted to the Church so that all Christians may know God; here we can have the power to sing: 'We have seen the true Light; we have received the Heavenly Spirit; we have found the true Faith, in worshipping the indivisible Trinity: for He hath saved us.'[76] This text expresses in a few words what this feast is about; the baptized are enlightened by the Spirit, and they recognize the saving God precisely in his worship – faith in the Trinity is not a matter of puzzling out a mathematical conundrum, but of living it out in the worship of the Church and in our daily lives.

The Vespers readings (from Numbers 11, Joel 2, and Ezekiel 36) relate the call of the elders to assist Moses, the pouring out of the Spirit of prophecy on God's people, and the promise of a new heart and new spirit in God's people. The Matins gospel and the epistle (John 20:19–23 and Acts 2:1–11) are about receiving the Holy Spirit; the gospel at the Liturgy (John 7:37–52 and 8:12) is the passage that begins 'On the last day of the feast . . .', it ends with the promise of the light of life for all who follow Jesus and receive the Spirit. The *troparion* stresses the gift of the Spirit to the fishermen[77] – it is through human beings that God now draws the world into his net; human beings who must pray for the spiritual gifts: 'Heavenly King, O Comforter, the Spirit of truth, Who art everywhere present and fillest all things, O Treasury of every good and Bestower of life: come and dwell in us, and cleanse us from every stain, and save our souls, O Good One.'[78]

It is customary to decorate the churches with greenery for Pentecost, and in some places (especially Ukraine) this is a day whereon green vestments are worn if the church possesses them. 'You and I have adorned this church with green branches in honour of this festival. We must adorn our hearts too, so that the fire of the Holy Spirit will descend on them.'[79] This Sunday really may be said to be a celebration of our share in God's Trinitarian life; but we continue to ask for the Spirit in our lives in the intense prayer that follows at Vespers. The next day is the Monday of the Holy Spirit, and in some cases, the Vespers may follow directly upon the Sunday liturgy.

This Vespers has additional prayers for the outpouring of the Spirit in the opening litany; the *stichera* sing of the Spirit of life and light, fountain of wisdom and understanding.[80] There now come, interspersed with the rest of the service, some lengthy prayers known as the Kneeling Prayers, for throughout the Fifty Days kneeling is strictly forbidden, and is only begun again now with these prayers. Unlike a lot of such prayers they are chanted aloud. The first expresses deep penitence and prays for forgiveness; the second prays for the gifts of the Spirit's wisdom to do good and live well, the third prays for the departed, and the fourth that we may walk in God's light; three others, ancient evening prayers, follow the first, second, and third.[81]

The Matins of Monday is a celebration of the gifts of the Holy Spirit as life to God's Church, the epistle (Ephesians 5:9–19) describes life in the Spirit, and the gospel (Matthew 18:10–20) concludes with the reminder that Christ is present where his people are gathered in his name. The Church is formed by the power of the Spirit, and that power is a power in a community who do God's will. The *Pentecostarion* finishes on the next Sunday, the Sunday of All Saints. The readings again show us the message of the day; the Vespers readings are all to do with the witness of holy people to God (Isaiah 43:9–14; Wisdom 3:1–9; Wisdom 5:15–6:3), the epistle is from Hebrews, the great cloud of witnesses; and the gospel is from Matthew 10 and 19, the call to take up one's cross and follow Christ. This is the Byzantine tradition's All Saints feast, but unlike the Western 1st November feast, celebrated as the last of the Easter observances.

We have not had a 'renewal of baptismal vows' like that of the modern Western Easter services, but, having celebrated the resurrection, reflected on the meaning of baptism, and prayed for the Holy Spirit in the life of the Church which we all share, we now go forward to lead that life, as far as possible inspired by the saints whose holy lives we try to emulate, because they too were sustained as we are, by the waters of rebirth, with the outpoured Spirit, and in the reception of the mystery of Communion in Christ's Body and Blood – yes indeed; 'We have seen the True Light.'

Wisdom from the East?

Is all that has been rehearsed above entirely foreign to Western Christians, or are there areas that might inspire new approaches and perspectives? An important first consideration would be the baptismal aspect of the Easter festival. As in the West, Easter was a baptismal season, perhaps the biggest of those seasons, but it does not seem to have ever been the only baptismal season. As was mentioned above, Pascha and Pentecost are joined by Christmas and Theophany in being festivals when baptisms might take place. This should not cause undue surprise; many early Christian writers, such as St Ephrem, appear to know of no exclusive connection between baptism and Pasch; several early liturgical descriptions, such as that of the *Didache*,[82] and that of Justin Martyr[83] do not mention any special season; and Tertullian in the third century saw Passover as the day of most solemnity for baptism, but by no means the only day.[84] In this case, it seems unwise to allow the baptismal aspect of the Paschal festival to overshadow everything else, at least, where that baptismal aspect seems to be largely to do with initiating new Christians.

There is a baptismal aspect to the whole of Christian life; in the Eastern tradition, prayer at sunset might be seen as entry into the tomb with Christ, so as to emerge into the light at sunrise. That daily cycle is intensified at the weekend, at the Saturday to Sunday services which find their climax in the Divine Liturgy, and even more intensified in the whole Lent and Easter cycle, with its deep reflection on sin, repentance, and suffering through the Great Fast and Holy Week; which then emerges into the life-giving light of the Risen Christ who sends the Spirit to inspire and animate the life of God's people. The message of this kind of Christian initiation is that one is initiated more by *doing* it, not so much by *learning* it – which means it is not only about other people who may or may not be becoming Christians, but is also always about me.

There will always be Christians whose attendance at church services is infrequent or perfunctory; there will also be Christians whose grasp of the Gospel is tenuous in the extreme; but the daily, weekly, and annual cycles should always be there as witness and inspiration that people may find are ready to inspire and animate them, if they are celebrated with a real sense of their power and potential appeal. There is no specific renewal of baptismal vows in the Byzantine tradition; rather, if one really shares in the worshipping life of the Church, that baptism is renewed again and again, and becomes the means by which we live our lives in the world in service of God and love of our fellows.

Another aspect that has been hinted at is the importance of food. Many people in modern Western societies have adopted a vegetarian diet for a wide variety of reasons, frequently ecological. The cycle of fast and feast can be a constant reminder that we are dependant on others in this creation, and ultimately dependant upon God. Since this is not a discussion on Lent, it is better to emphasize here the other side of the fast, the feast. Like all good feasts, they are much better shared with others; also the foods are appreciated the more if they have not been taken for some time. Some Christians give the impression that Lent is the only real season – but we need to celebrate as well! What better way than to have a party? Many churches of the Eastern traditions have a parish breakfast at Easter, or a parish party later in the day. The West had a tradition of eating certain foods at Easter, especially lamb; perhaps such things need some sort of revival.

Something else that some might want to give thought to is the employment of dramatic ceremonial such as the changing of vestments and hangings. To many, this sort of ceremonial seems vulgarly theatrical – and badly done, that is exactly what it is; done in a less self-conscious and more informal manner, these things can be powerful and moving, concrete expressions of all we are singing and saying. Some of the less official expressions of liturgical change require ease of movement by large groups of people. Also, the expectation that people will go in procession, will (in Lent) prostrate frequently, and so on, all this requires churches that, if provided with seating, make sure that it is far more flexible than the fixed aspect seating that now dominates all the churches of the Western denominations, and which has spread to some Eastern ones as well.

Marking out change in visual, audible, and tactile terms is not the only way of signalling such change. It is common in the East to use different incenses for different days; the Greek *Paschalia* incense has a very rich flowery aroma, quite distinct from the funereal heaviness of that used on Good Friday. The olfactory sense is not much used in Western Christianity; in the East, where people may well burn incense as part of their private prayers, it plays a much larger part, so incense can be bought in street stalls in, for example, Athens.

Greetings are also important. A Westerner may find it quite disconcerting to hear somebody ringing up a radio phone-in programme and start by saying '*Christos anesti!*', 'Christ is risen!' Amongst Ukrainians and others it is common to use seasonal greetings; at Christmas, the greeting 'Christ is born!' will elicit the reply: 'Glorify him', and at ordinary times, 'Glory be to Jesus Christ!'; and its reply, 'Glory for ever!' may well replace the time of day. These greetings can be heard all around, and may well be on the lips of those who were not in church; but even if they were not, the truth expressed is in the public forum – and yes, that should embarrass!

Particular observances of Byzantine Easter may also have a message for the West. The Slavonic feast of *Radonitsa* is a reminder of our hope of resurrection for all who have gone before us in death.[85] The Mid-Pentecost blessing of water, and the idea that one should bless the crops with that water is a powerful reminder that our Christian spring festival also commemorates the coming to new life of all the creation, the life of which we share. Above all, Ascension, which has become very downgraded in the West, is an important turning point, for we must come to terms with Christ's being away from us in one sense, and yet amongst us his people, in the power of the Spirit; which Spirit is calling us to be mature Christians who can be icons of Christ in the world of today.

Finally, the kneeling prayers at Pentecost are a reminder that posture is important. In Eastern churches where a choir or cantor execute the chants, one might be misled into thinking that there is no active participation. The Western fixation with verbal expression can blind people to what is going on about them. People might cross themselves at every petition in a litany; they are not perhaps singing 'Lord have mercy' but are they still not participating? The ancient prohibition of kneeling throughout Eastertide, or on any Sunday (including those of the Great Fast), goes back to the Council of Nicaea, and should cause us to be aware that we are all part of the priestly people of the Risen Christ.

Again, all that has been described really requires not only priests and deacons, but servers, choir and/or cantors, readers, people who will deal with lights and hangings, and people who will clean the church, all usually unordained, often female. Participation is more than a group of people saying or even singing words together.

Many people are struck by the formality and yet relaxed ordinariness of Byzantine worship; this is, at least partly, because the people as a whole feel that it is theirs, and not just a private possession of the clergy. A priest cannot celebrate Divine Liturgy alone (as can still happen in Roman Catholic circles), he always needs some people, so it is never 'his' liturgy. Neither priest nor people have the right to alter the services to suit their perceived needs and advantages; though there are a range of traditional adaptations.

At root, the Byzantine liturgical tradition is not so much about self-expression, as it is about joining in the common expression of that faith we share with our brothers and sisters, Catholic and Orthodox, throughout the world now, and through time; the faith that 'Christ is risen from the dead, trampling down death by death; and upon those in the tombs bestowing life!'

NOTES

1   This is an omnibus term for people whose ancestors came from the Carpathian mountain region of present-day Ukraine, Slovakia, and Hungary. Most have been in communion with Rome since the eighteenth century.

2   A *troparion* is a single stanza of religious poetry; many now stand alone as the typical proper chants of a particular feast or day.

3   The term 'Byzantine' is used here to designate all those, Orthodox and Catholic, who have in common the liturgical, spiritual and theological tradition that originates in Constantinople.

4   We shall refer throughout to the page numbers of the English edition (with some modifications of the language), Holy Transfiguration Monastery, Boston, Massachusetts (1990).

5   *Hesperinos* (Gk), *Vechernya* (Slavonic), the evening service, on Saturday night starts with Psalm 103 (104), then a litany and the reading from the Psalms. The evening psalms, 140 (141), 141 (142), 129 (130), and 116 (117) have poetic verses intercalated, called *stichera*; then comes the hymn 'Hail gladdening light' and some psalm verses, the *Prokeimenon*. Two further litanies and a prayer are followed by some more *stichera* (relics of an ancient procession) and the *Nunc Dimittis*. The final prayers include the Lord's Prayer, and the *troparion* of the feast. For fuller details, see Mother Mary and Archimandrite Kallistos Ware, *The Festal Menaion* (London: Faber & Faber, 1969), pp. 38–97.

6   *Orthros* (Gk), *Utrenya* (Sl) is much longer and rather complex. After an opening service with two psalms, come the fixed six Psalms (3, 37 (38), 62 (83), 87 (88), 102 (103), 142 (143)), a litany and some psalm verses. The reading from the psalter is followed on Sundays and feasts by the *Polyeleos*, Psalms 134–5 (135–6), and other chants before the gospel (on all Sundays, one of eleven resurrection gospels). After Psalm 50 (51) comes the canon; eight sets of *troparia* (originally nine scriptural canticles), between the eighth and the ninth the *Magnificat* is normally sung. Then comes the *Exaposteilarion* (intended to greet the rising sun as a symbol of the Risen Christ), and Psalms 148–50 with *stichera*. The festal office is completed by the Great Doxology ('Glory to God in the highest'), two litanies and prayer.

7   A good overview of the history may be found in R. F. Taft, *The Byzantine Rite: A Short History* (Collegeville, Minnesota: The Liturgical Press, 1992), esp. pp. 56–60.

8   See Taft on *Triodion* and *Pentecostarion* in A. P. Kazhdan (ed.), *The Oxford Dictionary of Byzantium 3* (New York–Oxford: Oxford University Press, 1991), pp. 1627 and 2118–9.

9   Texts in Mother Mary and Archimandrite Kallistos Ware *The Lenten Triodion* (London: Faber & Faber, 1978), pp. 655–660.

10 *Pentecostarion*, (Holy Transfiguration Monastery, Boston, Massachusetts, 1990) p. 27ff. The rubrics and texts for the midnight office that immediately precedes Easter Matins are found elsewhere.

11 G. Bertonière, *The Historical Development of the Easter Vigil and Related Services in the Greek Church* (Rome: Orientalia Christiana Analecta 193, 1972).

12 The *Typicon* (the book by which services are ordered) says the tenth hour of the day, see Mother Mary and Archimandrite Kallistos, *The Lenten Triodion*, p. 655.

13 G. Bertonière, op. cit., pp. 287–8 and 299–300.

14 Mother Mary and Archimandrite Kallistos op. cit., p. 655. There is no hard and fast colour sequence in the East, but white, or other bright light colours, are required for Easter and the whole Easter season. Dark vestments can mean black in some places, dark red in others.

15 Ibid., p. 656.

16   J. Mateos, *Le Typicon de la Grande Église II*, (*Orientalia Christiana Analecta 166*, 1963), pp. 84–8.

17   P. Lazar (ed.), *Great and Holy Saturday, Vespers and Divine Liturgy of St Basil the Great* (Latham NY: Dept. of Religious Formation, Orthodox Church of America, 1986), pp. 33–6.

18   Alexis Kniazeff identifies the first two readings as part of an ordinary daily cycle, the next four are Paschal, then six alternate between Paschal and baptismal, the last three being baptismal. 'La lecture de l'ancien et du nouveau Testament dans le rite Byzantin' in Bishop Cassian and B. Botte, (eds.) *La prière des heures* (Lex Orandi 35, Paris: Cerf., 1963), pp. 201–51, 218.

19   Lazar, op. cit., pp. 55–7.

20   Mateos, op. cit., pp. 88–9.

21   Lazar, op. cit., pp. 60–2.

22   Mother Mary and Archimandrite Kallistos, op. cit., p. 659.

23   Once the ordinary Sunday liturgy in Constantinople, it is now used only on ten days in the year (viz., Christmas Eve, Theophany Eve, St Basil's Day [1st January], the five Sundays of the Great Fast, Holy Thursday and Holy Saturday). The general structure is the same as the Chrysostom liturgy, but the presbyteral prayers, especially the Anaphora, are much longer.

24   Mother Mary and Archimandrite Kallistos, op. cit., p. 660.

25   P. Lazor, *The Paschal Service* (OCA, 1990), p. 9. It should not be necessary to point out that we are *all* children of those who were saved – this must not be interpreted in an anti-Jewish manner.

26   Mother Mary and Archimandrite Kallistos, op. cit., p. 660.

27   G. L. Papadeas (ed.), *Greek Orthodox Holy Week and Easter Services* (Daytona Beach Florida: Patmos Press, 1989), p. 448.

28   Lazor, *The Paschal Service*, pp. 25–6.

29   Psalms were sung in the tenth century, see Mateos, op. cit., p. 93ff.

30   Codex Jerusalem Patriarchate Hagios Stavros 43, see Bertonière, op. cit., pp. 12–18.

31   Ibid., pp. 94–7.

32   E.g., *New English Hymnal*, number 117 (Norwich: Canterbury Press, 1986).

33   Mary Sackville Lawson (ed.), *Collected Hymns and Sequences of John Mason Neale D.D.* (London: Hodder & Stoughton, 1914), p. 233 (the whole canon is found at pages 231–6).

34   A hymn originally sung by both choirs together in the centre of the church.

35   *Pentecostarion*, p. 29.

36   Ibid., p. 31.

37   Ibid. Sung at Sunday Matins after the resurrection Gospel, and also, daily until Ascension before Psalm 50.

38   Ibid., p. 33.

39   Ibid.

40   Ibid., p. 35.

41   Ibid., p. 36.

42   Or in many Greek churches, just before the empty Good Friday sepulchre, which now has flowers and an icon of the resurrection in it.

43   In Greek usage, this sermon is commonly read at the end of the Liturgy that follows Matins; Papadeas, op. cit., pp. 481–2.

44   This is made up of poetic pieces from the other services, and has no psalms – it is also sung in place of Compline and the Midnight office, see *Pentecostarion* pp. 37–8.

45   The traditional fast excludes meat, fish and dairy products throughout Lent – oil and wine, traditional signs of joy, may be used on Saturdays and Sundays.

46   These latter details I owe to Bishop Kallistos (Ware) of Diokleia.

47   The eight tones comprise related melodies for the main classes of hymns.

48   The resurrection hymns for the Sunday services are found in the liturgical book called the *Oktoechos*, or 'Book of Eight Tones'. Those who are interested can find a selection of *stichera*, the *troparia* and *kontakia*, and the *irmosy* of the canon in I. F. Hapgood (ed.), *Service-Book of the Holy Orthodox–Catholic Apostolic Church* (Englewood, NJ: Antiochian Orthodox Christian Archdiocese of New York and All America, 1975, 5th edition), pp. 577–91. Archbishop J. Raya and Baron J. de Vinck, *Byzantine Daily Worship* (Allendale NJ: Alleluia Press, 1969), pp. 123–149.

49   *Pentecostarion*, p. 42.

50   Mateos, op. cit., p. 97ff. This tenth-century document requires the singing of the same *Prokeimena* as today, in the same order.

51 For further details of this process, R. F. Taft, *The Liturgy of the Hours in East and West* (Collegeville, Minnesota: The Liturgical Press, 1986), pp. 273–7.
52 Papadeas, op. cit., pp. 491–4.
53 C. Protopresbyter Papayiannis (ed.), *I Agia kai Megali Evdomas*, (Athens: Apostoliki Diakonia, 1990), pp. 377–98.
54 Chrismation, or Confirmation, is an integral part of the Baptismal rite, as is the reception of Holy Communion; which means that infants are communicants from their baptism onwards.
55 *Pentecostarion*, p. 51.
56 Ibid., p. 52.
57 Ibid., p. 55.
58 Ibid., p. 29.
59 Revelation is not read liturgically in Byzantine tradition. See the convenient scheme of the reading cycle in Casimir Kucharek, *The Byzantine-Slav Liturgy of St John Chrysostom* (Allendale, NJ: Alleluia Press, 1971), p. 443.
60 Ibid., p. 422 for overview of the cycle, detailed for John's gospel, pp. 440–1.
61 Obviously a great part of this reading takes place on weekdays; those unable to attend each day are encouraged to read the epistle and gospel for the day at home.
62 Ibid., p. 440.
63 Further detail and explanation in A. Schmemann *Great Lent* (Crestwood, NY: St Vladimir's Seminary Press, 1974), pp. 67–76. [We refer to the 'Great Fast' in distinction to the other fasting seasons; Lent is old English for spring.]
64 *Pentecostarion*, p. 68.
65 Ibid., p. 75.
66 Hapgood, op. cit., p. 28.
67 *Pentecostarion*, p. 165.
68 *Pentecostarion*, p. 191.
69 Ibid., p. 219.
70 See, A Monk of the Eastern Church (i.e., Archimandrite Lev Gillet), *The Year of Grace of the Lord* (Crestwood, NY: St Vladimir's Seminary Press, 1992), pp. 190ff.
71 The Greater Blessing is that done at Theophany (Epiphany), which is even more explicitly baptismal in its imagery, see Kallistos Ware and Mother Mary, *The Festal Menaion* op. cit., pp. 348–58.
72 *Pentecostarion*, p. 278.
73 *Pentecostarion*, p. 323.
74 Ibid., pp. 327–8.
75 Ibid., pp. 361–2.
76 Ibid., p. 404. This hymn is also sung after Communion (except during Eastertide) at all liturgies.
77 Ibid., p. 407.
78 Ibid. A frequently used prayer to the Holy Spirit, e.g., it is used at the beginning of every service outside of Eastertide.
79 From a sermon for Trinity Sunday by the late Father Alexander Men, *Awake to Life* (London: The Bowerdean Press, 1992), p. 89.
80 *Pentecostarion*, pp. 418–20.
81 Ibid., pp. 420–6.
82 E. C. Whitaker, *Documents of the Baptismal Liturgy* (London: SPCK), p. 1.
83 Ibid., p. 2.
84 Ibid., p. 9.
85 The author did know of a Roman Catholic parish in the north of England that sang Mass on Easter Monday in the local cemetery chapel – a very similar idea.

RISE HEART: CHURCH MUSIC IN THE EASTER SEASON

Rise heart; thy Lord is risen. Sing his praise
     Without delays,
Who takes thee by the hand, that thou likewise
     With him mayst rise:
That, as his death calcined thee to dust,
His life may make thee gold, and much more just.

Awake, my lute, and struggle for thy part
     With all thy art.
The cross taught all wood to resound his name,
     Who bore the same.
His stretched sinews taught all strings, what key
Is best to celebrate this most high day.

Consort both heart and lute, and twist a song
     Pleasant and long:
Or since all music is but three parts vied
     And multiplied;
O let thy blessed Spirit bear a part,
And make up our defects with his sweet art.

I got me flowers to straw thy way;
I got me boughs off many a tree:
But thou wast up by break of day,
And brought'st thy sweets along with thee.

The Sunne arising in the East,
Though he give light, & th' East perfume;
If they should offer to contest
With thy arising, they presume.

Can there be any day but this,
Though many sunnes to shine endeavour?
We count three hundred, but we misse:
There is but one, and that one ever.

George Herbert's poem 'Easter', expressing as it does the great surge of joy at the Gospel of Easter after the long darkness of Holy Week, might well be a manifesto for the church musician in the Easter season. 'Awake my lute, and struggle for the part with all thy art . . . Consort both heart and lute, and twist a song pleasant and long.' Few would demur from the suggestion that the Easter season of fifty days is the season *par excellence* for music making in the church, for we are an Easter people, and 'Alleluia' is our song. That, at least, is the theory!

The reality, in my own experience and that of the church musicians with whom I have worked, is that often as not Easter morning is greeted with a sigh of relief: the struggle of Lent and Holy Week is over for another year, and things can now get back to normal. The Triduum may well be a liturgical and musical high point in the year, but it is also demanding and exhausting for musicians and clergy alike. Little wonder then that the great Fifty Days between Easter and Pentecost often get off to a bad start, treated by church musicians as a gap in which to draw breath before the further exertions of Ascension Day and Pentecost.

This desire to honour the season while at the same time acknowledging the human need to pause for breath is a tension with which church musicians and all servants of the liturgy need to grapple. It means, in practical terms, making as much time to plan what happens after Easter Day as is given to what leads up to it. No one expects that the intensity of the Vigil or of Easter morning will be sustained for the whole period up to Pentecost, for its intensity is largely dependent upon contrast with what has gone before. But this Easter season is no short interlude between great festivals: it is in total about one seventh of the Church's year, often referred to by liturgists and others as the 'Year's Sunday',[1] and as such it should be the time for particular celebration. The exultant shout of 'Alleluia!' inevitably has a different quality as the season progresses. This is not a measure of failure. The season is one in which the breadth of the Paschal Mystery is explored and celebrated by the assembly – one in which the startling twist of the Easter narrative of the tomb gives way to the Church's narrative of the Risen Lord who dwells with her. The task of the musician is to work with the other liturgy planners to provide continuity and cohesion in this great celebration.

What follows is intended to be a resource for musicians and others. It is intended neither to be prescriptive nor exhaustive, for the nature of church music making is that in each situation there are different demands, different resources and indeed different models of the very role of music in the liturgy. Many groups may have a much more developed idea of how Easter can be honoured musically. But for others the ideas that follow may help to stimulate or refine their planning.

Some principles of musical planning for the season

Planning in groups

The first thing is a *crie de cœur*! Having worked on both sides of the great divide fixed between church musicians and the clergy I am convinced that successful liturgy planning can only be done collaboratively. If liturgy is about the people of God celebrating the life of God then autocratic liturgical planning by the *fiat* of either clergy or musicians will inevitably fall short of what might have been achieved had those responsible for words, music, movement, reading and preaching got together. This move towards more collaborative planning requires humility and tact, and an investment of time: in short a real commitment to the liturgy of the Church, but I am convinced that it is the only way to get the liturgy right. In more and more congregations the planning of the liturgical life of the assembly is being done by groups consisting of liturgical professionals (clergy, musicians and others) and lay people, and it is increasingly being done on a seasonal basis. In this way the entirety of a season can be planned. What are the themes of the season, both in the readings from the Scriptures and in the life of the local or wider community? What hymns or service music (or dance, or non-scriptural words or even silence!) can be chosen to help in the celebration and exploration of these themes? How should we decorate the church for the season?

And what of the wider life of the community: study groups, concerts, trips and social events – how can all these be fused together? If we are prepared to accept that often the liturgy of the Church is used by people as a forum in which they can 'do their own thing' (and how guilty are both musicians and clergy of that!), and set ourselves to work collaboratively to counteract individualism and party interest, and genuinely to celebrate through our worship the life of God in the people of God, we will be nine-tenths of the way there. And the goodwill of church musicians is an essential prerequisite.

Studying the art of the possible

It is axiomatic that no church musician is ever satisfied with things as they are! If only we had more resources, more time, better support, how much better things could be. And yet the true art of the church musician is to make best use of what wide and varied talents which already exist. 'Blessed be the God and Father of our Lord Jesus Christ', S. S. Wesley's oft-sung anthem, beloved of organists for its magnificent crashing B flat dominant seventh before the final fugal section, was written during Wesley's time as organist of Hereford Cathedral for an Easter Day in the early 1830s on which 'only Trebles and a single Bass voice'[2] (according to one version of the story, the bishop's butler) were available. It is a fine example of mastery of the art of the possible, and of creative resourcefulness. In all the suggestions which follow, mastery of the art of the possible is essential. Nothing is worse, nor more detrimental to worship, than hearing overtaxed singers struggling through an over-ambitious programme, and so where a church choir exists realistic choices have to be made, for the sake of everyone. We have to stretch music to fit the people, not the other way round.

Perhaps, though, this has more profound implications than we realize. It may well be that within congregations there are also musical skills and abilities long neglected. Part of our total celebration in the liturgy may well be using those gifts in the course of worship. At a basic level it may simply be a desire to sing (which may necessitate popularizing the choice of hymns and songs), or an ability to play a musical instrument (which may call for the formation of a church orchestra or music group). It may well be that there are people available who could act as cantor for responsorial music, or who could join a simple congregational choir to give a lead in sung responses. All such initiatives beg questions of the 'professional' church musician about the relationship between music as offering or art form and music as pastoral tool, and the answers may not necessarily be to everyone's liking. We church musicians have a tendency to build empires, empires which we defy well-intention pastoral-hearted people to undermine. Yet the sacrifice of self-interest for the wider good may be one which is demanded of us, and as the Church moves increasingly away from a clergy-dominated model towards a more collaborative and pastoral model, perhaps musicians have to fact the fact that the task which music faces is also changing. Music may have to be less of a feature of an Easter parade than a tool for building up an Easter people.

Seeking balance and restraint

It may seem odd in a chapter which seeks to encourage the music of Easter to suggest that we should sing less. The art of good liturgical planning, rather like the planning of a good meal, lies in getting the balance between all the different component parts right, and as often as not for the musician this may well mean having less music than might be possible for the sake of the overall balance. It very much depends what the role of music is: whether it is there 'because we always have it there', or whether it is there because it has a clear function within the liturgy. Each church's view of this will be different, dictated by the sort of musical foundation it has, and the style of the worship it enjoys. In an abbey church with an able robed RSCM-affiliated choir there may well be a case for using music differently from the way in which it might be used in a city housing estate church with a scanty musical tradition. There are no absolutes. What above all is to be avoided is the idea that sung liturgy is 'better' than said liturgy, or that the more music you have the better.

What is important is not that the music should be plentiful, but that it should be effective in the given situation – and I suspect that a general rule might be that if we concentrated on singing less music better we might end up with better liturgy. Nothing alienates a congregation more than an excess of tiresome, badly performed music. Far better to have a text declaimed well by a reader, than have everyone cringing as it is massacred by a singer, or inept member of the clergy. Sensitive musicians will have to be bold and inventive at the planning stage if they are to contribute to this successful balance, and they may well have to adopt the unusual stance of suggesting that 'just because it was sung last year, it needn't be this year'. Paradoxically, showing restraint in musical provision in the short term may be precisely the way, in the long term, to achieve more and better musical involvement among the people of God.

So, three principles established, on to some detailed suggestions for the season of Easter.

The service music of the season

The Vigil and First Eucharist

Of the essence of the drama of the Easter Vigil is *contrast*. In the Service of Light the light of the candle shines amid the darkness, the proclamation of the Easter message resounds in the silence of the church, and the singing of the *Gloria in excelsis* is greeted with organ fanfares and, in some places, the ringing of bells. This stark drama is easy to subvert, unwittingly, by inappropriate musical settings or by poor handling of the reading of the Old Testament Prophecies, but simply and well handled it can be a striking experience.

The first question for the planning group is that of the shape of the service. It is possible to have the Prophecies[3] as part of a Vigil Service before the Service of Light, or alternatively (my own preference) to have them after the Service of Light in an extended Liturgy of the Word. If the former option is chosen (perhaps because there is a suitable place in which to gather for a Vigil), the musician, in setting the psalms which accompany the readings, will have to be careful not to pre-empt the centrepiece of the Easter Proclamation, the *Exultet*. Perhaps better, for this reason, to begin outside the church with the Service of Light. Then the contrast between the simple proclamation 'The light of Christ' and the *Exultet*'s great cascade of florid plainsong is heightened. Whichever shape is decided on, there are perhaps five major musical points to consider:

1 Carrying the Paschal candle and the *Exultet*.
2 The reading of the Prophecies with their accompanying psalms and canticles.
3 The singing of the *Gloria*.
4 The singing of the Alleluia which greets the gospel of Easter.
5 Music for a procession to the font.
6 The Proper Dismissal at the end of the eucharist.

1   The Paschal candle and the *Exultet* – proclaiming the Light of Christ. The proclamation of the Light of Christ is best done simply, using the following response:

PROCLAIMING THE LIGHT OF CHRIST

> The following simple response should be sung
> on a slightly higher starting note each time.

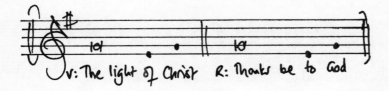

Source: trad

Its simplicity then makes a great contrast with the proclamation of the *Exultet*. This great lyrical prayer, properly sung by the deacon after the Paschal candle has been carried into the church and placed in a prominent position, has its roots in the ancient Gallican liturgy, and has been a standard part of the Easter rite of the Western Church since the Middle Ages. In some places it has been sung with particular solemnity, the music being sung from a great cascading scroll of parchment, often highly decorated. The *Exultet* itself falls into two main sections: the first, *Exultet jam angelica turba* (Rejoice heavenly powers, sing choirs of angels), proclaiming the mystery of Easter, and the second a prayer consecrating the candle, introduced by the familiar *Sursum corda* dialogue of the eucharistic liturgy. If the history of the chant is complex,[4] it is as nothing compared with the presumed complexity of the chant as a piece of music to be performed, the nightmare of many a deacon! In fact there is nothing to say that the traditional plainsong version of the *Exultet must* be sung, and there is no point in its being attempted if there are more musically edifying options. It may well be that with the growth in popularity of responsorial service music there are good reasons for preferring a responsorial version of the *Exultet*, or perhaps a metrical setting sung like a hymn to a well-known tune will the better enable people to share in the proclamation of the light of Christ. The following are two suggestions for a 'traditional' and a 'responsorial' Exultet, and *Lent, Holy Week, Easter (LHWE)* also has a metrical version for congregational singing to the tune Woodlands (*New English Hymnal* No. 395).

A TRADITIONAL EXULTET

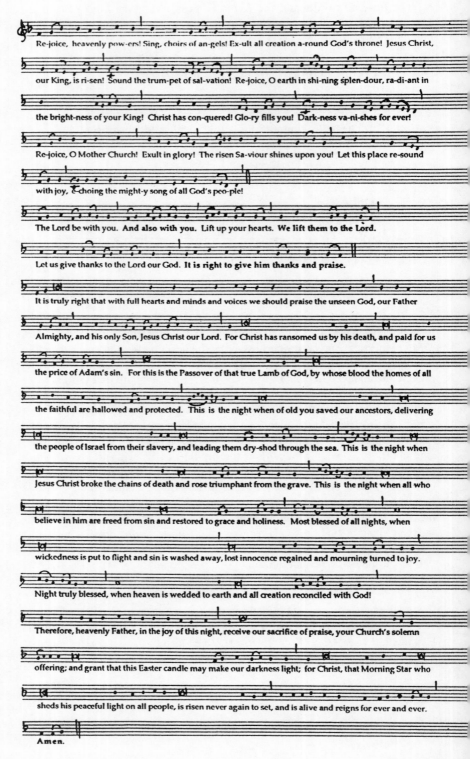

Re-joice, heavenly pow-ers! Sing, choirs of an-gels! Ex-ult all creation a-round God's throne! Jesus Christ,

our King, is ri-sen! Sound the trum-pet of sal-vation! Re-joice, O earth in shi-ning splen-dour, ra-di-ant in

the bright-ness of your King! Christ has con-quered! Glo-ry fills you! Dark-ness va-ni-shes for ever!

Re-joice, O Mother Church! Exult in glory! The risen Sa-viour shines upon you! Let this place re-sound

with joy, e-choing the might-y song of all God's peo-ple!

The Lord be with you. And also with you. Lift up your hearts. We lift them to the Lord.

Let us give thanks to the Lord our God. It is right to give him thanks and praise.

It is truly right that with full hearts and minds and voices we should praise the unseen God, our Father

Almighty, and his only Son, Jesus Christ our Lord. For Christ has ransomed us by his death, and paid for us

the price of Adam's sin. For this is the Passover of that true Lamb of God, by whose blood the homes of all

the faithful are hallowed and protected. This is the night when of old you saved our ancestors, delivering

the people of Israel from their slavery, and leading them dry-shod through the sea. This is the night when

Jesus Christ broke the chains of death and rose triumphant from the grave. This is the night when all who

believe in him are freed from sin and restored to grace and holiness. Most blessed of all nights, when

wickedness is put to flight and sin is washed away, lost innocence regained and mourning turned to joy.

Night truly blessed, when heaven is wedded to earth and all creation reconciled with God!

Therefore, heavenly Father, in the joy of this night, receive our sacrifice of praise, your Church's solemn

offering; and grant that this Easter candle may make our darkness light; for Christ, that Morning Star who

sheds his peaceful light on all people, is risen never again to set, and is alive and reigns for ever and ever.

Amen.

Source: t

A RESPONSORIAL EXULTET

> In this form of the Exultet the first part can
> be sung by cantor and congregation, and
> then the minister can take up the spoken
> part at 'The Lord be with you...'

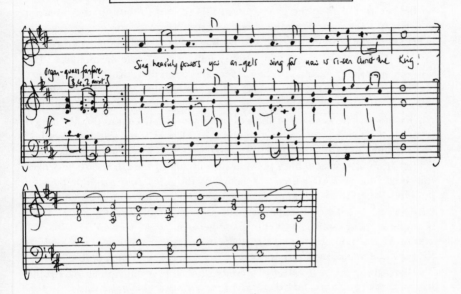

Response: Sing heav'nly powers, you angels, sing! For now is risen Christ the King

1. Sing you heavens! Choirs of angels, rejoice!
   Let all created things now with them sing.
   With blast of trumpets tell the news abroad,
   That Jesus Christ is risen, our Lord and King. (Response)

2. His light is shed abroad through all the earth;
   The brightness of the splendour of our King;
   Death is now conquered, darkness is ended.
   Of his triumphant glory let us sing. (Response)

3. And we his people, holy Church, rejoice!
   The light of Christ shines on us from on high.
   Around the world the Church raises her voice;
   Our hymns and songs and psalms proclaim our joy! (Response)

Spoken: The Lord be with you
And also with you

Lift up your hearts
We lift them to the Lord.

Let us give thanks to the Lord our God.
It is right to give him thanks and praise.

It is indeed right that with full hearts and minds and voices... *etc*

2 The readings in the Vigil/Liturgy of the Word – celebrating God's saving acts.

Section 48 of *LHWE* provides a wide range of readings from the Old and New Testaments suitable for inclusion in a Vigil or extended Liturgy of the Word on Easter Eve. Not all of these need be read (there are in total some fourteen readings including the gospel), and indeed the need to sustain the drama of the Liturgy of the Word might make the reading of five or six plus a gospel a better option. In planning the execution of this part of the liturgy the musician will have to have an eye to the overall pace of the proceedings; the repeated cycle of reading–psalm–prayer will be the better if planned silence is used creatively, and if there are no unsightly gaps where none are planned. This will mean proper rehearsal of the readers and the musicians involved.

The music of this section should not be over-ambitious. The now popular responsorial psalm/canticle form is what is suggested in *LHWE*, and this allows the people to share in the liturgy. There are dramatic possibilities in some of the words, not least in the *Song of Moses* from Exodus 15 which accompanies the fifth reading – but restraint should be shown so as not to detract from the musical high point of the singing of the *Gloria*. As a general rule an 8' flute should be used to accompany the solo cantor, with perhaps the judicious addition of a 4' stop in unison congregational responses. Otherwise why not use a piano or a guitar, or perhaps even sing unaccompanied? There is ample scope for musical inventiveness here, but what is essential is that this section is not overblown, and that the cantor is well rehearsed and ready to lead the congregation in responses which are simple and memorable.

There are many suggestions for suitable psalm arrangements by Brother Reginald SSF in *Lent, Holy Week and Easter: music for the services*[5] and the majority of other Responsorial Psalm books have sections on the Psalms of the Easter Vigil and for the rest of the Easter season. Among these are: *A Responsorial Psalm Book*,[6] '*Ways of Singing the Psalms*',[7] *A Responsorial Psalter*[8] and *Psalms for the Church's Year*.[9]

3 Singing the Gloria.

The *Gloria* should not normally be sung from Ash Wednesday for the entire duration of Lent, and so its welcome return at the First Eucharist of Easter can be a special high point. The musical setting used should probably be one familiar to the congregation, and ideally a congregational setting rather than a choir piece. Particularly appropriate would be something like the festal arrangement of *The People's Mass* by Dom Gregory Murray, or perhaps the increasingly popular 'Lourdes Gloria' with its simple and memorable response. In many churches there is the practice of ringing bells (which have been silent throughout the Triduum) and sounding organ fanfares after the *Gloria* has been intoned, and even letting off party poppers. To the uninitiated that may sound excess of the worst sort, but if the Vigil/Liturgy of the Word has been well handled the effect can be truly uplifting. Be bold: try it!

4   The Alleluia – greeting the Easter gospel.

'Alleluia' is the cry that resounds through the whole narrative of Easter, and so it is proper that it should be emphasized at the very beginning of Eastertide. If the singing of an Alleluia is regularly part of the liturgy in a church, it should have been dropped for the duration of Lent, and hymns with 'Alleulias' in them should have been avoided. This is an ancient practice, and in medieval plainsong books long alternatives to the Alleluia (called Tracts) were provided for use in Lent. The Alleluia might well be used after the New Testament reading as the gospeller prepares to read the gospel. How best this should be done will be for the planning committee to work out, but again perhaps a responsorial arrangement with the congregation repeating what a cantor has first sung to them is best, with the cantor then singing an appropriate sentence before the Alleluia is repeated. The two examples below are simple arrangements of traditional Alleluia melodies, the second traditionally sung at Easter. In addition there is the increasingly popular 'Celtic Alleluia' by O'Carroll & Walker.[10]

EASTER ALLELUIAS

Source: ©Alan Gyle

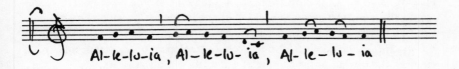

Source: trad

5   A procession to the font.

Easter Eve is traditionally the time when catachumens are welcomed into the church in the rites of initiation. Whether or not there are people to be baptized *LHWE* suggests a renewal of baptismal vows by all present (sections 25ff) and this may necessitate the provision of some music to cover the move to the font. Simplest may be the singing of a hymn. John Mason Neale's baptismal hymn 'With Christ we share a mystic grave' is singularly appropriate in its use of the imagery of the rites of initiation, but perhaps with people on the move something better known might work better. A responsorial setting of Psalm 42 ('As the running deer seeks the flowing brooks') sung in procession would be very suitable, as would the traditional Litany of the Saints. If the Renewal of Baptismal Vows is followed by the Peace, then a suitable offertory hymn (perhaps with a few moments of improvization beforehand) will neatly cover the return to the altar if such is necessary.

6   The Proper Dismissal.

The following is the traditional dismissal for the eucharist throughout the Easter season.

EASTER DISMISSAL

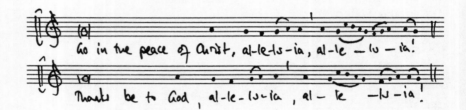

Source: trad

The eucharists of the Easter season

The Vigil and First Eucharist of Easter set the tone for the whole of the Easter season till Pentecost, and so some of what has been suggested above for the Vigil and First Eucharist will be relevant to the planning of other liturgies. Hymnody and Psalmody will be covered as a separate item later, and so, in the meantime, what of the service music of the Easter season?

The Penitential Rite in the Easter season

In its section of Supplementary Texts, *LHWE* provides a seasonal form for the Penitential Rite. This, in common with other such forms, uses a congregational Kyrie/Christe response after seasonal sentences. Since the *Gloria* will be sung throughout the season, a sung form of the penitential rite might help to introduce a seasonal flavour into the opening of the service. Something like the following, suitably transposed to fit in with the key of the *Gloria* might form a basis.

Confessions
Resurrection, Heaven, Glory, Transfiguration, Death, Funerals

Cantor:

O Je - sus Christ, ri - sen mas - ter and tri - um - phant Lord, we come to you in sor - row for

our sins, and con - fess to you our weak - ness and un - bel - ief:

We have lived by our own strength, and not by the power of your re - sur - rec - tion.

In your mer - cy, for - give us:

treble
alto

Lord,   hear   us   and   help   us.

congregation/
choir II

Lord, _____

Lord,   hear   us   and   help   us.

tenor
bass

We have lived by the light of our own eyes, as faith - less and not be - liev - ing.

In your mer - cy, for - give us:

CELEBRATING THE EASTER MYSTERY

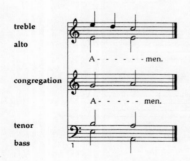

The Alleluia

This is an absolute prerequisite throughout the season, and here is a selection of possible forms. Beware of the temptation to change things too often: better to select one Alleluia melody and stick to it until it is thoroughly familiar. The

51

Plate 1.
Anastasis: Russian; late
16th century.
Reproduced by
permission of The
Temple Gallery

Plate 2.
Anastasis and
Ascension, from a
Church feasts icon:
Novgorod region; early
16th century.
Reproduced by
permission of The
Temple Gallery

Plate 3.   Mid-Pentecost: Novgorod; 15th century. Reproduced
by permission of The Temple Gallery.

Source: ©John P. Kitchen, used with permission

Intercessions

What too of the idea of using a litany form for the intercessions during the season? *Patterns for Worship*[11] provides various seasonally appropriate forms, which readily lend themselves to musical setting.

The Peace

One other trick of the trade to mark this season out as different is to introduce music during the sharing of the Peace (if such takes place). How precisely this is done will depend on the local resources available, but introducing, say, an improvised crescendo as soon as the Peace begins, leading into the playover of an Offertory hymn can provide a subtle uplift to what is sometimes a slightly awkward moment. It is perhaps the sort of thing that can become a cliché if done too often, but it might well help to mark out the festal character for the Sundays of Easter, particularly after the more sombre celebrations of Lent.

Voluntaries and other music before and after services

Whether the music in a church is provided by an organist or by a music group it hardly needs to be pointed out that there is a wealth of seasonally appropriate music for the Easter season. Organists in particular might like perhaps to play some seasonal chorale prelude; if so, why not have it put down on the pew sheet or weekly bulletin? For some of the uninitiated the music before and after services is just like wallpaper music – liturgical muzak. Others, though, set great store by what is played, and so if the music has an Easter theme then why not spell that out? And if organists or musicians are going to the trouble of playing appropriate music, the clergy and worship leaders, inevitably getting ready behind the scenes, could do much to encourage a more reflective and prayerful hearing. A note or an announcement encouraging people to listen to the 'beauty and teaching of the music' might just do the trick.

Hymnody in the Easter season

The choosing of hymns and psalms for worship is one of the most important tasks that forms part of liturgy planning. In the singing of hymns the majority of people learn the vocabulary of their faith and in singing together they are called into participation in worship and learn the language of the Christian community. It should, for that reason, be no surprise that feelings run high where hymn choice is concerned. Most of the music suggested so far has been service music, for the simple reason that involving the congregation in active participation in the liturgy is a priority; but now to the hymns of Eastertide.

Hymn choice in the Easter (or indeed in any) season will be governed by a number of factors, the first and most significant of which is perhaps the readings chosen for the Sundays. There are at present two major lectionaries in use. The first, familiar from the *ASB*, is a two-year cycle which is thematic (e.g. the second Sunday after Easter has as its theme either The Good Shepherd or the Emmaus Road depending on which is the current year of the cycle). The other major lectionary is that derived from the Roman Missal, the so-called *Common Lectionary*, which functions on a three-year Sunday cycle, years A, B and C. This second lectionary reads the gospels *in course* rather than in thematic chunks. The Gospel of the day, together with suggested other readings and Psalmody will suggest possible hymns, some of which may, for example, use scriptural imagery.

Beyond this, hymn choice will be dictated by musical common sense: how long, what mood, what tempo? By and large Entry hymns and Offertory hymns may have a significant amount of liturgical action to cover, whereas a Gradual or post-Communion hymns may have a different function. There is also the basic fact that as the mood of the season changes, i.e. the nearer we get to Pentecost, so too must the mood of the hymns: 'Jesus Christ is risen today!' is probably more appropriate towards the beginning of the season than towards the end. Finally there is the observation that not all the hymns for Easter need necessarily come from the 'Easter' section of the hymn book!

Depending on what lectionary is in use, musicians and liturgy planning committees have a number of resources to draw on:

1   The major hymn books (e.g. *New English Hymnal*, *Celebration Hymnal* and *A&M* (New Standard)) have, at the back, suggested hymns for seasons (and even for particular Sunday themes).
2   A number of quarterly Liturgy Planners are published (e.g. as a supplement to the Society of St Gregory's periodical *Music & Liturgy* or in the *Southward Liturgy Bulletin* – both Roman Catholic publications) and these have suggested hymns for individual days, drawn from a wide variety of hymn books and other sources, as well as a wide selection of other liturgical suggestions.
3   Mowbrays publish a companion volume to the *ASB*: *A Hymn Guide for the Sunday Themes of the New Lectionary in the ASB 1980*.

In selecting hymns do read right through the words: often the opening lines of hymns in Liturgy Planners don't reveal what the link is. Take time to plan, but do use the resources available: there is no point in reinventing the wheel!

Other music in the Easter season

Finally, it would be wrong to give the impression that the only place for music is in the eucharists of Easter. Family Services and Daily Prayer should also have a highly seasonal flavour. Outside the regular round of services, and with a bit of imagination, there may well be many other ways in which music can play a part in marking out the season as one of celebration and exploration. The lessons-and-carols model, familiar to us from the Christmas season, could well be adapted for an Easter Festival – and this might be the sort of more flexible one-off event that could involve more fringe members of the community. A form for such a celebration, entitled 'an Easter Sequence', is included in this volume. On a smaller scale, more meditative series of reflections about the mystery of Easter might use taped or live music. The local choral society might be dissuaded from singing Part II of The Messiah in Lent, and instead be encouraged to sing Part III in the Easter season. It might also be possible in some places to arrange an Easter season recital or music programme in a church building, where the emphasis in the publicity could be on the distinctive character of the season, with appropriate music.

In celebrating Easter the ministry of the church musician is absolutely vital. Where there is trust and mutual respect between musicians and other liturgical professionals, and where imagination and a bit of creativity are in evidence, music can contribute towards giving the whole of the season a unity and a momentum, in which the 'Alleluia!' of the Church can ring out to the glory of God.

NOTES

1 This expression has become widely used since its incorporation in a Roman Catholic circular letter entitled *Celebrating Easter*, published by The Congregation for Divine Worship in 1988 (CTS Do580).
2 Nicholas Temperley, 'Samuel Sebastian Wesley' in *The New Grove Dictionary of Music and Musicians*, ed. Stanley Sadie, (Macmillan, 1980), vol. 20.
3 For a liturgy for the Easter Vigil see *Lent, Holy Week, Easter: Services and Prayers*, (CHP/SPCK/CUP, 1984), pp. 228ff. The so-called 'Prophecies' are given at section 48, together with accompanying Psalms and prayers.
4 For a full treatment of the literary and musical structure of the *Exultet* see Michel Huglo, 'Exultet' in the *New Grove*, vol. 6, pp. 334ff.
5 I. Forrester, (ed.), London, McCrimmon, 1988.
6 G. Boulton Smith, (ed.), London, Collins, 1980.
7 Leaver, Mann and Parkes (eds), London, Collins, 1984.
8 Texts© *The Psalms: a new translation*, London, McCrimmon, 1987.
9 Publ. in UK by Decani Music, Suffolk; in US by GIA Publications, Chicago.
10 © Sinton O'Carrol and Christopher Walker. Published in UK by Kalmus, and administered by Decani Music, Suffolk; in US, publ. by OCP (Oregon Catholic Press), 5536 N. E. Hassalo, Portland, OR 97213.
11 *Patterns for Worship*, London: Church House Publishing, 1995.

6

AN EASTER SEQUENCE OF READINGS AND MUSIC

This proposed Easter Sequence is a reflective Evening Service of words and music for the Easter season. It proclaims the resurrection of Jesus Christ, and by its structure of thematically arranged readings, prayers, hymns and anthems gradually unfolds the mystery of how God, even now, raises us up with Christ and works his Easter miracle in those who are joined to Christ.

The Service of Light

The ministers enter with the Paschal candle, which is set up in the centre of the nave.

Acclamation:

> O Christ, the light of the world. Alleluia, alleluia.
> **You dispel the darkness of our hearts and minds. Alleluia, alleluia.**

Prayer for the blessing of the Light:

> Blessed are you, Lord our God,
> our alpha and omega, our beginning and our end,
> for you have raised Christ the first-fruits from the dead
> to be our light and our hope.
> In the knowledge of his resurrection
> may we follow all that is good, and just, and true,
> and through our Easter celebration
> glimpse that celestial city where there is
> neither light of lamp, nor sun,
> but the eternal glory of our transformed humanity,
> in the mutual love of the Father, Son and Holy Spirit.
> **Blessed be God for ever!**

Or,

Let us give thanks to the Lord our God.
It is right to offer thanks and praise.

We give you praise and glory, sovereign God,
for in vindicating your Son,
you have made our darkness to be bright.
Through the power of the Spirit you raise us up
with Christ to be children of light.
In the abundance of your grace,
revealed in the face of Jesus Christ,
may we welcome the stranger,
and face all we meet with trust and truth;
that the whole world may be filled
with your ever unfolding love.
Through Christ, and in the Holy Spirit,
we offer you all praise, and honour, and worship,
now, and until the end of the ages. **Amen.**

The Word of God

Rise up, O children of light, and let us give glory to the Lord, who
gives life to our mortal bodies.
**May we contemplate God's wondrous work with awe, and
worthily proclaim his praise.**

THE EASTER HAPPENING

(*choir*)

'This joyful Easter tide' (arr. Philip Ledger) from David's Psalmer
(1685),
or, 'Christ the Lord is Risen today' (John Rutter).

Readings:

either, Luke 24:1–10; or Matthew 28:1–10, and one of the following:
George Herbert 'Easter Wings'; or
Elizabeth Jennings 'Easter Morning'.

Hymn (one of the following):

'Lord of the Dance' (Sydney Carter) NEH 375.
'The Day of Resurrection' (St John of Damascus) NEH 117.
'Now the green blade riseth' (J. M. C. Crum) NEH 115.

Celebrating the Easter Mystery

GOD'S EASTER IN US

Readings:

> 'Good Friday 1613, Riding Westward' (John Donne)
> and 2 Corinthians 4:7–end.

Responsory:

> I have been crucified with Christ.
> **It is no longer I who live, but Christ who dwells within me.**
>
> You must count yourself dead to sin and alive to God in Jesus
> Christ our Lord.
> **I have been crucified with Christ.**
>
> Glory to the Father, and to the Son, and to the Holy Spirit.
> **It is no longer I who live, but Christ who dwells within me.**
>
> As in Adam all die,
> **So in Christ shall all be made alive.**

Collect:

> Grant, O Lord of Life,
> that as we have been baptized into the death of your beloved Son,
> our Saviour Jesus Christ,
> so by his conversion of our misdirected desires, and selfish
> inclinations
> may we die to sin and be buried with him,
> that through the grave and gate of death
> we may pass to our joyful resurrection;
> through him who died, was buried,
> and raised by the power of the Spirit,
> your Son, Jesus Christ our Lord.[1]

Hymn:

> 'With Christ we share a mystic grave' NEH 317.

THE EASTER LIFE

Readings:

> John 20:19–24 or Ephesians 4:1–13.

Organ interlude

One of the following, or some other non-biblical reading:

'Pax' (D. H. Lawrence).
'Immortal Joy' (Kathleen Raine).
'As Kingfishers Catch Fire' (G. M. Hopkins).

Silence may be kept for a space

Hymn:

'Breathe, on me, Breath of God' (E. Hatch) NEH 342.
or some other suitable hymn.

Prayers of intercession for the Church and the world

Response to each bidding:

Risen and glorious Christ.
Come among us, restore and remake us.

Forgiving Lord, you restored Peter into fellowship and call us all to
be one people: take from our hearts the spirit of retaliation; grant us
the grace to forgive others, and the desire to build community with
those with whom we live, and work, and worship.

Risen and glorious Christ.
Come among us, restore and remake us.

Ascended Lord, you gather up all things in heaven and earth; grant
to all who govern the nations, and those who shape and implement
economic and social policy a vision of the new Jerusalem, that our
lives may be peaceably and justly ordered, and all people dwell in
freedom and integrity.

Risen and glorious Christ,
Come among us, restore and remake us.

Living Lord, you meet us with your abundance and call us into the
fullness of life; hear our prayer for those who lack food and clean
water, and prosper the work of those who bring relief to those in
need.

Risen and glorious Christ,
Come among us, restore and remake us.

Lord of all life, in your risen body you bear the marks of suffering; look with compassion upon all who are maimed and scarred by the violence of others. Speak your word of peace and dispell the anxiety of those bearing physical pain, and those suffering mental anguish.

Risen and glorious Christ,
Come among us, restore and remake us.

First born of the new creation, strengthen with your Spirit those who in this season have been joined to you in baptism, and incorporated into your Body the Church; through your grace may the fruits of the Spirit come to maturity in our lives, and may all our prayers and praises be joined to the prayers and praises of the saints in light.

Risen and glorious Christ,
Come among us, restore and remake us.

Collect:

God our redeemer and our strength,
the risen Christ breathed the spirit
upon the first disciples in the Upper Room.
Shower that same Spirit upon us,
and fill us with your energies and life,
your gifts of hope and joy;
that being undaunted by terrors and trials,
we might promote your peace,
and ever marvel in the rich diversity of your world.
We ask this in the name of Jesus Christ our Lord.

The Lord's Prayer:

Our Father in heaven,
hallowed be your name,
your kingdom come,
your will be done,
on earth as in heaven.
Give us today our daily bread.
Forgive us our sins
as we forgive those who sin against us.
Lead us not into temptation
but deliver us from evil.
[For the kingdom, the power,
and the glory are yours
now and for ever.] **Amen.**

The Blessing:

> May Christ, the Sun of Righteousness,
> who rekindles the fire of love,
> and opens a new horizon of hope,
> awaken you to new life;
> and the blessing of God almighty,
> the Father, the Son, and the Holy Spirit,
> be among you, and remain with you always.
> **Amen.**

Final hymn:

> 'Thine be the glory' (Edmund Budry) NEH 120,
> or some other rousing hymn.

NOTE

1   BCP adapted.

7

THE VIGIL OF THE RESURRECTION

The Vigil of the Resurrection is a short night service to be celebrated on Saturday nights. At its heart is the proclamation of the Easter Gospel, and as such is preparatory for Sunday, that 'little Easter' which begins each week. It is envisaged that the service might take place in the chancel of a church, or chapel, with the Paschal candle being placed in front of a lectern in the centre of the chancel. Those who gather to celebrate this Vigil might be given individual tapers, or candles, but only the Paschal candle is lit before the service begins. It would be desirable if the service was conducted in subdued lighting. The people should assemble and take their places in silence.

The minister, led by an assistant, enters in silence, and sits in the sanctuary, preferably before the altar and facing down the chancel.

> Our help is in the name of the Lord,
> **Who has made heaven and earth.**
>
> **Glory to the Father, and to the Son, and to the Holy Spirit;**
> **as it was in the beginning, is now,**
> **and shall be for ever. Amen. Alleluia!**

The following, or some other suitable hymn is sung:

> *Vexilla Regis prodeunt*
>
> The royal banners forward go,
> The cross shines forth in mystic glow,
> Where he in flesh, our flesh who made,
> Our sentence bore, our ransom paid.
>
> Fulfilled is all that David told
> In true prophetic song of old,
> The universal Lord is he,
> Who reigns and triumphs from the tree.

To thee, eternal Three in One,
Let homage meet by all be done:
Whom by thy Cross thou dost restore,
Preserve and govern evermore. Amen.

(*Latin, Venantius Fortunatus 530–609, Tr. J. M. Neale 1818–66*)

Prayer of Thanksgiving for the Light

The light and peace of Christ Jesus be with you all.
And also with you.

Let us give thanks to the Lord our God.
Who is worthy of all thanksgiving and praise.

Blessed are you, Sovereign God of all,
to you be praise and glory for ever!
In raising your Son from the dark caverns of death
you have made manifest a light which shall never fade;
in that light may we see ways of rebuilding
a world fractured and disfigured by violence,
remembering that without your saving help our labour is in vain,
for you are the architect of that abiding city of peace,
and through the indwelling of the Spirit
make our bodies to be temples to your glory,
blessed and glorious Trinity,
Father, Son, and Holy Spirit.
Blessed be God for ever!

PSALM 118:

1 Give thanks to the Lord, for he is good;
His mercy endures for ever.

2 Let Israel now proclaim;
His mercy endures for ever.

3 Let the house of Aaron now proclaim;
His mercy endures for ever.

4 Let those who fear the Lord now proclaim;
His mercy endures for ever.

5 I called to the Lord in my distress;
the Lord answered by setting me free.

6 The Lord is at my side, therefore I will not fear;
what can anyone do to me?

7 The Lord is at my side to help me;
I will triumph over those who hate me.

8 It is better to rely on the Lord
than to put any trust in flesh.

9 It is better to rely on the Lord
than to put any trust in rulers.

10 All the ungodly encompass me;
in the name of the Lord I will repel them.

11 They hem me in, they hem me in on every side;
in the name of the Lord I will repay them.

12 They swarm about me like bees;
they blaze like a fire of thorns;
in the name of the Lord I will repel them.

13 I was pressed so hard that I almost fell,
but the Lord came to my help.

14 The Lord is my strength and my song,
and he has become my salvation.

15 There is a sound of exultation and victory
in the tents of the righteous:

16 'The right hand of the Lord has triumphed!
the right hand of the Lord is exalted!
the right hand of the Lord has triumphed!'

17 I shall not die, but live,
and declare the works of the Lord.

18 The Lord has punished me sorely,
but he did not hand me over to death.

19 Open for me the gates of righteousness;
I will enter them; I will offer thanks to the Lord.

20 'This is the gate of the Lord;
he who is righteous may enter.'

21 I will give thanks to you, for you answered me
and have become my salvation.

22 The same stone which the builders rejected
has become my chief corner stone.

23 This is the Lord's doing,
and it is marvellous in our eyes.

24 On this day the Lord has acted;
    we will rejoice and be glad in it.

25 Hosanna, Lord, hosanna!
    Lord, send us now success.

26 Blessed is he who comes in the name of the Lord;
    we bless you from the house of the Lord.

27 God is the Lord; he has shined upon us;
    form a procession with branches
    up to the horns of the altar.

28 'You are my God and I will thank you;
    you are my God and I will exalt you.'

29 Give thanks to the Lord, for he is good;
    his mercy endures for ever.

Psalm Collect

God the source and fulfilment of our life,
you make us to be living stones
built together into a temple to your glory,
with Christ Jesus its cornerstone;
purge and purify our hearts and minds
that we may enter the gates of righteousness,
and offer a sacrifice of praise worthy of your holy name,
through him who was victim,
and who now ever lives to make intercession for us,
Jesus Christ, our Saviour and High Priest.
Amen.

Canticle

Either, the Song of Moses and Miriam (Cantemus Domino), or the Easter Anthems.

The Song of Moses and Miriam:

Refrain:

**In your unfailing love, O Lord,
you lead the people whom you have redeemed.**

I will sing to the Lord, who has triumphed gloriously;
the horse and the rider have been thrown into the sea.

The Lord is my strength and my song,
and has become my salvation.

This is my God whom I will praise;
the God of my ancestors whom I will exalt.

The Lord fights for his people;
the Lord is his name.

Your right hand, O Lord, is glorious in power:
your right hand, O Lord, shatters the enemy.

At the blast of your nostrils, the sea covered them;
they sank as lead in the mighty waters.

In your unfailing love, O Lord,
you lead the people whom you have redeemed,

And by your invincible strength
you will guide them to your dwelling.

You will bring them in and plant them, O Lord,
in the sanctuary which your hands have established.

**Glory to the Father, and to the Son,
and to the Holy Spirit:
As it was in the beginning, is now,
and shall be for ever. Amen.**

THE EASTER ANTHEMS:

Christ our passover has been sacrificed for us,
so let us celebrate the feast,

Not with the old leaven of malice and wickedness
but with the unleavened bread of sincerity and truth.

Christ once raised from the dead dies no more;
death has no more dominion over him.

In dying, he died to sin once for all;
in living, he lives to God.

See yourselves, therefore, as dead to sin
and alive to God in Jesus Christ our Lord.

Christ has been raised from the dead;
the first fruits of those who sleep.

For since by one man came death,
by another has come also the resurrection of the dead,

For as in Adam all die;
even so in Christ shall all be made alive.

Glory be to the Father, and to the Son,
and to the Holy Spirit;
As it was in the beginning, is now,
and shall be for ever. Amen.

The Gospel of the Resurrection

An Alleluia chant is sung as the minister approaches the lectern to read one
of the Easter Gospels. The individual tapers are lit during the singing to greet
the Gospel, and incense may be offered as a memorial of the aromatic spices
brought by the women to the tomb of Jesus on the first Easter Day.

The Gospel is announced in the customary way, and the following passages
are suggested for use: John 20:1–18; Matthew 28:1–10; Mark 16:1–8; Luke
24:1–12.

After the Gospel has been declaimed, the following acclamation may be said,
or preferably sung:

To you be praise, to you be thanksgiving,
glory be to you, blessed Trinity,
Father, Son and Holy Spirit.

Silence may be kept for reflection.

The Prayers

As we await a new day, let us pray for the dawning of God's kingdom in the words our Saviour Christ gave us:

Our Father ...

THE COLLECT OF THE RESURRECTION:

Lord of creation and redeemer of all,
through the resurrection of your Son
you have dispelled our darkness
by the brilliance of your one true light;
kindle within us the fire of your love
that we may radiate your heavenly glory,
and with pure hearts attain the feast of everlasting light;
through Jesus Christ our Lord,

who lives and reigns with you and the Holy Spirit,
one God, now and for ever.
Amen.

May the crucified and Risen Lord bestow upon us
his Easter gifts of joy and peace.
Amen.

Let us bless the Lord. Alleluia! Alleluia!
Thanks be to God. Alleluia! Alleluia!

ORTHODOX ICONS FOR THE EASTER SEASON

'Christ is risen from the dead, trampling down death by death, and upon those in the tomb bestowing life.'[1] This text rings out through the Orthodox celebration of Easter. Not only is Christ's own resurrection being celebrated in terms of victory over death, but also the opening of new life for all humanity. The event and its implications are celebrated together in a way that is typical of the whole pattern of Orthodox liturgical celebration. The cycle of the feasts and fasts is not a tangled skein of temporal events but rather a complex tapestry within which we are taken through a celebration of the work of God and invited to relish the implications of the love which comes to share and transfigure our humanity. As with the rest of the liturgical cycle, so particularly with the period of Easter to Pentecost there is a profound inter-relationship between the feasts. This is most obvious when we see how the celebration of the Ascension looks forward to Pentecost, and the celebration of Pentecost in its turn takes our attention both into the mystery of the Trinity and into the mystery of the Church.

It is important to recognize that the faith of the Orthodox Christian Tradition is expressed in both verbal and visual language. There is the verbal language of Scripture, of the writings and homilies of the great theologians of the Church, and of the liturgical texts which express the Church's faith in worship. And there is the visual language of the icons and wall paintings that are so conspicuous in Orthodox churches. The two languages are inter-related, and these two aspects of tradition interact with each other over the centuries as the Church continues to reflect on and worship within the celebration of these central mysteries of the faith.

The scriptural and liturgical texts, and the icons associated with Easter, the Ascension and Pentecost all echo the Church's praise from within the experience of redemption and sanctification. They express Christian faith and experience from within the context of worship. The Church does not so much understand the mystery of redemption and sanctification as celebrate the mystery: the mystery of what God has done, is still doing, and will bring to fulfilment. The language of poetry, imagery and symbolism has a conspicuous place in the celebration of this mystery which is beyond human comprehension. Within this celebration we can recognize the different strands of dogmatic, ecclesial, spiritual and liturgical theology, as part of the full texture of the faith, but the reality is integrated within the prayer of the Church. In this respect, the Orthodox Church continues to honour the saying of Evagrius, 'If you are a theologian you truly pray. If you truly pray you are a theologian.'[2] In this tradition, theology and prayer cannot be treated as separate matters.

When we look at an Orthodox icon associated with the celebration of Easter, what do we expect to see? If we come from a Western background, we may well expect some illustration of Christ coming from the tomb, the soldiers asleep or frightened by the earthquake, or people like St John, St Peter and St Mary Magdalene visiting the tomb. Some Orthodox icons do in fact show the spice-bearing women at the tomb, emphasizing the emptiness of the tomb. However, the main icon associated with Easter is very different.

The icon generally referred to as 'The Anastasis' (The Resurrection) is a sophisticated theological image that seems to have begun its development in the Byzantine world in the eighth century; during later centuries considerable further developments have taken place, and several variations of this central Easter icon can be seen across the broad expanse of Orthodox history and geography. Yet in spite of great variations the central elements in the icon remain conspicuous in their consistency: Christ is shown descending into Hades to rescue Adam and Eve. Christ the Second Adam descends to the depths to rescue the first Adam. Christ the Redeemer enters the underworld to free those held captive by the powers of darkness and death. This central and dramatic truth of Christ's work of redemption is consistently set forth in the Anastasis icon (Plates 1 and 2).

The imagery of this icon is derived in part from Scripture, from such New Testament texts as these: David 'foresaw and spoke of the resurrection of the Christ, that he was not abandoned to Hades, nor did his flesh see corruption. This Jesus God raised up, and of that we all are witnesses' (Acts 2:31–2). 'For Christ also died for sins once for all, the righteous for the unrighteous, that he might bring us to God, being put to death in the flesh but made alive in the spirit; in which he went and preached to the spirits in prison' (1 Peter 3:18–19). Of greater significance in the development of the Anastasis icon is the rich tradition of homilies expounding the Easter Mystery; in this tradition poetry and a sense of drama, historical event and its wider significance all become woven together into an eloquent exposition of the drama of salvation. The purpose of the homily is to move the listeners to active faith, and to enrich their awareness of the mystery that is at the heart of the liturgical celebration. To this day the Easter sermon ascribed to St John Chrysostom forms part of the liturgy of Easter. The use of scriptural allusion and imagery is vivid, as is the strong sense of drama and the victory of Christ over the powers of darkness:

Let all take part in the banquet of faith. Let all take part in the wealth of righteousness. Let no one lament for poverty, for the kingdom is made manifest for all. Let no one bewail transgressions, for forgiveness has dawned from the tomb. Let no one be fearful of Death, for the death of the Saviour has set us free. He has quenched it by being subdued by it. He who came down into Hades, despoiled Hades; and Hades was embittered when it tasted of his flesh. Isaiah, anticipating this, cried and said: 'Hades was embittered when below it met thee face to face.' It was embittered for it was rendered void. It was embittered for it was mocked. It was embittered for it was slain. It was embittered for it was despoiled. It was embittered for it was fettered. It received a body, and encountered God. It received mortal dust, and met heaven face to face. It received what it saw, and fell whither it saw not. O Death, where is thy sting? O Hades, where is thy victory? Christ is risen and thou art overthrown. Christ is risen and the demons have fallen. Christ is risen and the angels rejoice. Christ is risen and freedom is given to life. Christ is risen and there is none dead in the tomb. For Christ is risen from the dead, and become the first-fruits of them that slept. To him be glory and power from all ages to all ages. Amen.[3]

How more dramatic could be the affirmation of what was accomplished in Christ's descent? Hades 'received a body, and encountered God. It received mortal dust, and met heaven face to face'. In the depths of the underworld Christ's work of redemption is continued. The crucifixion on Calvary is not the final abasement of Christ in the Incarnation. The final abasement is to the depths of Hades, and from those depths Christ arises, not alone, but bringing up Adam and Eve into new life. This celebration of the raising of Adam and Eve comes as the climax of the Lenten and Holy Week observances in which the fall of Adam is persistently lamented, not simply as a past event, but as a continuing human fall from God in which we all are implicated; the cry that God will 'Call back Adam' is a cry that the whole of humanity may be brought into Paradise, freed from sin, and transfigured in Christ. The accomplishment of this redemption is anticipated on the third Sunday of Lent, the Sunday of the Adoration of the Precious and Lifegiving Cross: 'This is a day of festival: at the awakening of Christ, death has fled away and the light of life has dawned; Adam has arisen and dances for joy.'[4] In the Anastasis icons we see the accomplishment of redemption: 'The gates of death have opened unto thee in fear, O Lord, and the doorkeepers of Hades quaked when they saw thee. For thou hast shattered the gates of brass and smitten the bars of iron in sunder. Thou hast led us out of darkness and the shadow of death, and broken our bonds.'[5] 'Adam, who fell and has been raised up, was terrified when God walked in paradise, but rejoices when he descends into Hades.'[6]

In some of the Anastasis icons a figure personifying Hades is shown bound in the depths of the earth, with Christ trampling him down, and raising Adam from the grasp of Hades. In most panel icons, however, the figure of Hades does not appear. A diffidence about representing a conspicuous personification of death or the underworld seems to have led to the removal of Hades from the scene in icons which were meant for veneration. Instead, the broken gates of Hades, the locks and chains of the underworld, and the tombs of Adam and Eve occupy the lower levels of the icon. From the depths Christ raises Adam; sometimes Eve also is shown being raised by Christ, but more frequently she is shown behind Adam in a posture of supplication, awaiting the attention of the Saviour. The rocky background in the icon is divided, as if echoing the division of the waters of the Red Sea in the Old Testament Passover. The figure of Christ is often clothed in a brilliant white garment, and surrounded by a mandorla; Christ usually holds a scroll or a cross in the left hand, while with his right hand he grasps the wrist of Adam and raises him up from the tomb and lifts him into the mandorla, thus signifying his redemption into the divine life. Other figures in the icons include David and Solomon, the royal forebears of Christ. Their presence in the icon affirms the humanity of Christ, and signifies the prophecy and wisdom that foresaw the Incarnation. The righteous dead who are often depicted include John the Baptist ('the Forerunner' in Orthodox terminology), and other prophets and kings from the Old Testament period.

The significance of the descent of Christ in the Incarnation is powerfully expressed by St Makarios of Egypt: 'What was the purpose of his descent to earth except to save sinners, to bring light to those in darkness, and life to the dead?'[7] It is this descent that we see in the Anastasis icon, the descent of Christ to the depths to accomplish the triumphant liberation of humanity from the bonds of sin and death, and its resurrection into the glory of God's kingdom.

At a point midway between Easter and Pentecost (on the Wednesday of the fourth week after Easter) the Orthodox Church keeps the feast of Mid-Pentecost. The Jewish festivals of Passover and Pentecost were highly significant for the early Church because of events in the life of Christ and his Church that had taken place at the time of the festivals: the death and resurrection of Christ at the time of the Passover festival, and the outpouring of the Holy Spirit at the time of Pentecost. The gospel reading for the feast of Mid-Pentecost (John 7:14–36) brings into focus the third of the Jewish festivals which had Messianic significance for the Christian Church: the feast of Tabernacles. According to chapter 7 of St John's gospel, Jesus went up to the temple at the middle of the feast of Tabernacles, and taught in the temple. His teaching there looks beyond his death and resurrection to the outpouring of the Holy Spirit: 'On the last day of the feast, the great day, Jesus stood up and proclaimed, "If any one thirst, let him come to me and drink. He who believes in me, as the scripture has said, 'Out of his heart shall flow rivers of living water.'" Now this he said about the Spirit, which those who believed in him were to receive; for as yet the Spirit had not been given, because Jesus was not yet glorified.' (John 7:37–9). It is this teaching that forms part of the gospel for the feast of Pentecost itself (John 7:37–52; 8:12).

The feast of Mid-Pentecost draws our attention to Christ's presence in the temple at the middle of the feast of Tabernacles; this incident and the festival at which it occurs are taken from their historical chronological sequence and remembered in Mid-Pentecost because of the role of Christ as teacher in the temple, and the teaching that foretells the gift of the Spirit.

The theme of 'living water' (John 7:37) is prominent in the celebration of Mid-Pentecost, but not in the icons of the feast. The icons of the feast are concerned with Christ's presence in the temple at the feast of Tabernacles as the teacher whose glorification through the cross will lead to the gift of the Spirit; they are also concerned with Christ's presence at the feast of Passover at the age of 12 (Luke 2:41–51), when he confounds the Jewish teachers with his understanding (Plate 3).

The icons thus bring together different incidents in the temple where the Divine Wisdom is manifested in the person of Christ. In the icon the youthful Christ-Emmanuel is seated at the centre of a group of six teachers; he is placed at a higher level in the icon than the teachers, and the whole group is set against the background of the temple. The architectural features of the temple have that peculiar non-naturalistic quality that is often present in Russian icons; these features serve to indicate the historical setting of the event in time and space, and also its significance beyond the confines of the particular time and place.

Christ is present teaching in the temple in Jerusalem as the 12-year-old youth and again later as the mature teacher of Divine Wisdom. But he also is the temple whose destruction leads to resurrection and glorification, and the outpouring of the Spirit. The icon of Mid-Pentecost has a very similar form and structure to the Pentecost icon of the descent of the Holy Spirit, and this fact serves to emphasize the inter-relationship of the themes involved in these two feasts.

The feast of Mid-Pentecost has no place in Western liturgical observance. The significance of the feast is not immediately obvious to people whose liturgical life has been shaped by a different tradition. However, for the Orthodox Church this feast is an important celebration of Christ as the Wisdom of God who is manifested in the temple, and whose prophecy of the descent of the Holy Spirit is fulfilled at the feast of Pentecost.

In the icons of the Ascension (Plate 2) the earthly scene is set on the Mount of Olives, as is implied in Scripture (Acts 1:12), and often shows the rocky mountain top and some olive trees. The group of figures in the earthly scene includes the apostles and the angels, and also the Mother of God. Although the Acts of the Apostles does not specifically mention her presence at the Ascension, Orthodox tradition has always assumed her presence there. St Luke certainly shows her as part of the Christian community that met together in the Upper Room after the Ascension. The Mother of God is usually shown in a central position, at the centre of the apostolic group; she is at the heart of the Church's life; she upon whom the Holy Spirit had descended at the Annunciation to bring about the Incarnation is now at the heart of the apostolic group; and it is upon this group that the Holy Spirit will descend at Pentecost to bestow new life and power to enable the Church to disperse from Jerusalem on the universal mission entrusted to it by Christ (Acts 1:8–9).

This centrality of the Mother of God in the earthly group means that she is placed immediately beneath the figure of the ascended Christ, whose Incarnation was made possible through her obedience. Thus the icon stresses not so much the separation of heaven and earth, but rather the union effected by the Incarnation.

> Having appeared in the likeness of the body, thou, O Lover of men, hast joined into one what was formerly separated, and in the sight of thy disciples, O Merciful One, thou didst go up into heaven.[8]

> Having accomplished the economy concerning us and united those on earth with the heavenly, thou hast ascended into glory, O Christ our God, being in no-wise separated, but remaining ever present and crying out to those that love thee: I am with you, and no one can prevail against you.[9]

In the upper level of the icon the figure of Christ is usually shown seated upon a rainbow, (plate 3) with a scroll in his left hand, and his right hand raised in blessing; angels support the mandorla within which the figure of Christ is placed. Thus the ascended Christ blesses the Church which is left on earth with the Mother of God at the heart of its praise and prayer. The raised hands of the Mother of God gather together the apostolic group in an attitude of attentive expectation that the promise of the Spirit will be fulfilled.

> The Lord hath ascended into heaven, that he may send the Comforter unto the world.[10]

> Being ascended up into heaven, whence also thou hadst come down, leave us not comfortless, O Lord. But let thy Spirit come, bearing peace unto the world, and show the works of thy might upon the sons of men, O Lord, who lovest mankind.[11]

As part of the Church on earth we join the heavenly powers in glorifying the Lover of mankind:

> We earthborn, glorifying thy condescension toward us and thine Ascension from us, pray saying: Do thou who at thine Ascension didst fill with joy unutterable thy disciples and the Birth-giver of God who bare thee vouchsafe unto us, thine elect, joy also, through their prayers, because of thy great mercy.[12]

78

Icons of the Ascension seem suffused with a sense of joy and expectancy: the grouping of the figures, the gestures of arms and hands, and the attitudes shown in the heads and faces all express joy at Christ's ascension. Adam has been sought out, found, and brought home; our humanity has been raised to the throne of God.

> Having sought out Adam that erred through the temptation of the serpent, thou, O Christ, as one who hath put him on, ascendedst and wast seated on the right hand of the Father . . . while angels hymned thee.[13]

> God is gone up with a shout, the Lord with the sound of a trumpet that He may exalt the fallen image of Adam and send down the Spirit the Comforter to hallow our souls.[14]

It is in this joy at the ascension of Christ that the Church lives and worships and awaits the promised return. The depiction of Christ in the icons of the Ascension is echoed in icons of the Last Judgment: the One who has ascended to the heavens is the One who will return as Judge, so the icon of the Ascension acts as a prophetic icon pointing us forward to Christ's Second Coming. 'This Jesus, who was taken up from you into heaven, will come in the same way as you saw him go into heaven' (Acts 1:11).

The celebration of Pentecost in the Orthodox tradition marks two related spiritual realities and events: first, the outpouring of the Holy Spirit on the Day of Pentecost and the continuing presence of the Spirit within the Church; and second, the full manifestation of the Trinity thus accomplished. The feast of Pentecost, therefore, celebrates the historical event of the gift of the Spirit, and at the same time forms the culmination of the other events which are seen as 'theophanies', namely the Baptism of Christ and his Transfiguration. In all three events there is a specific unfolding or revealing of the mystery of the Holy Trinity.

This twofold aspect of the feast of Pentecost is reflected in the two icons which are associated with the feast, the icons showing the descent of the Spirit, and the Trinity icon. The icon of the Holy Trinity is used on Pentecost Sunday, showing the feast to be a celebration of the Theophany – the manifestation of the mystery of the Holy Trinity. The icon of the Descent of the Spirit is used on the Monday after Pentecost.

Before looking in some detail at the Trinity icon, it is necessary to understand something of the theological discipline that lies behind the use of icons in the Orthodox Church. During the Iconoclast controversy in the eighth and ninth centuries the theology of icons was violently disputed and vigorously defended. The iconoclasts quoted the Old Testament prohibitions against the worship of graven images, and the condemnations of idolatry. The iconodules (those who defended the painting and veneration of icons) responded by stating that the prohibitions given in the Old Testament applied to the time before the Incarnation, to a period before God had been manifested in the flesh. 'No one has ever seen God,' says St John, 'the only Son, who is in the bosom of the Father, he has made him known' (John 1:18). Because God the Son had become incarnate in the person of Jesus Christ, the representation of the person of Christ in icons could be defended. So too could the veneration of the icons. They were not accorded the worship that is due to God alone, but a degree of veneration or honour appropriate to them as bearers both of truth revealed within the Church and also of worship offered through the Church. The defenders of the icons at the Seventh Ecumenical Council in 787 and in subsequent centuries stressed the person of Christ represented in icons, and the significance of the events in his life; they stressed the person of the Mother of God and her significance in the economy of salvation; and they stressed the persons of the saints who share in the transfigured, perfect humanity of Christ. Of course, over the centuries, there have been deviations from this rule, but the fundamental principles behind the Orthodox use of icons remain to this day those stated in the Council in 787.

In the light of this strict theological discipline, how does the Church create an icon that is appropriate for the celebration of the mystery of the Holy Trinity? The answer may seem rather complex, but it does have an inner consistency and directness once the dynamics of the theology have been grasped. The key to solving the problem lies in the understanding of the way revelation unfolds: something is foreshadowed, hints are given, and the way is prepared for a fuller manifestation. We are familiar with this process in relation to the theology of redemption: the work of Moses and the events of the Passover and the Exodus from Egypt in the Old Testament foreshadow the greater redemption and Passover accomplished by Christ through his death and resurrection. That is why the liturgy of Easter both in East and West contains so much of Holy Scripture that relates to the Passover.

In a similar way the Fathers of the Church have seen in the Old Testament other aspects of God's revelation which find fulfilment in the New Testament. From the fourth century onwards Christian writers saw in the story in Genesis 18 a foreshadowing of the revelation of the Holy Trinity. We are told that 'The Lord' appeared to Abraham at the oaks of Mamre, but we are also told that Abraham 'lifted up his eyes and looked, and behold, three men stood in front of him'. Abraham greets them as 'My Lord' and bows down before them prior to preparing a meal for these mysterious visitors. 'The Hospitality of Abraham', as this event is known, involves Abraham giving hospitality to three visitors, and later receiving the promise that Sarah will bear a son.

The scene is represented in Christian art from the late fourth century, and gradually finds its way to becoming one of the standard scenes that one can expect to see represented along with many other 'feeding scenes' from the Scriptures. In this scene the three visitors are represented as angels, winged beings, and Abraham and Sarah are involved in providing food; a tree is there to represent the oak of Mamre, a building represents the house or tent of

Abraham, and a mountain is often represented, possibly as a symbol of the meeting of God and man. This image develops in significance both in theological writings and in art. It becomes THE way of representing the mystery of the Trinity, a mystery foreshadowed in the meeting of the Lord and Abraham, but fulfilled in the revelation that comes with the Incarnation and Pentecost.

At the Baptism of Christ the Trinity is manifested in the voice of the Father, the descent of the Spirit in the form of a dove, and in the person of Christ the Son. Similarly at the Transfiguration, the Trinity is manifested in the voice of the Father, the cloud as a symbol of the Spirit, and the person of the Son in Jesus himself whose divinity is disclosed to Peter, James and John. At Pentecost the person of the Spirit is manifested in a way that completes and fulfils what was foreshadowed in the revelation to Abraham. So, although 'no one has ever seen God' there are events which provide the possibility of visual representation on the basis of 'typology': the earlier event is a 'type' or 'shadow' of the reality which is to be revealed later; the 'type' or 'shadow' provide a model or symbol by which the revelation can be communicated without falling into the trap of idolatry.

The Hospitality of Abraham in Christian art is one of many images involving feeding; it appears in Orthodox Churches along with the Last Supper, and is often associated with the celebration of the Eucharistic Liturgy. In the sixth-century church of San Vitale at Ravenna the mosaic of the Hospitality of Abraham is closely linked with the scene of Abraham's willingness to sacrifice Isaac, and with the offering of bread and wine by the priest-king Melchizedek. The themes of sacrifice and communion are closely inter-related.

It is interesting to note the transformation that takes place in the significance of this event. Genesis 18 tells of Abraham's hospitality to the three mysterious visitors, and then moves on to God's promise of a son to Abraham, whom Abraham will later be willing to offer in sacrifice. In the theological and iconographical tradition of the Church the event is transformed to become an image of the divine communion of the Holy Trinity into which we are drawn through the sacrificial death of the Incarnate Son. The process of theological development takes place over many years, and involves the drawing together of a great variety of theological truths and insights into one image. The image can speak in a very direct and intuitive way, but considerable theological discernment is required to see the full significance of this major theme in Orthodox iconography.

In almost all icons, mosaics and other images of the Hospitality of Abraham before the fifteenth century there is quite a full representation of the details of the story. Abraham and Sarah are shown; sometimes there is a servant slaying an animal; the table at which the angelic visitors are seated is often lavishly set with food; the oak of Mamre and the house or tent of Abraham are sometimes shown in great detail, and the mountain looks very realistic. In some icons it is possible to discern different ideas of how the three angelic beings relate to the persons of the Holy Trinity. In almost all icons it is very obviously a feeding scene – a sign of nourishment in its many forms, the sharing of life, and the establishment of communion (Plate 4).

The most famous icon of this tradition is the one that makes the most marked departure from the form that had been established for centuries. St Andrew Rublev was a Russian monk in the monastery established in the mid-fourteenth century by St Sergius some miles outside Moscow in the forest where he had spent many years as a hermit. St Sergius lived at the point in Russian history where there was a great danger that the whole spiritual heritage it had received from Byzantium might be destroyed under the increasing burden of Tartar oppression which was creating a serious fragmentation of Russian society. St Sergius was a great spiritual leader who had a profound impact on Russian society; his influence led to a recovery of confidence and a greater cohesion between the divided Russian princes, and a strengthening of nerve in the face of the oppressor. St Sergius came to be seen as the person whose vision and courage allowed Russia to emerge from a state of broken-ness and fear to become a nation with a strong sense of its spiritual vocation and responsibility. But we must not forget that St Sergius was a monk nur-tured in the hesychast tradition of prayer; his spiritual gifts led to the founda-tion of monastic communities, and at the heart of his life was a passionate devotion to the Holy Trinity.

In the biography of St Sergius written shortly after his death we read that he 'built the Church of the Holy Trinity as a mirror for his community, that through gazing at the Divine unity, they might overcome the hateful divisions of the world'. The contemplation of the mystery of the Holy Trinity seems to have been the key to the way that St Sergius triumphed over the hateful divi-sions of society in his own day and laid the spiritual foundations for the great flowering of Russian spirituality and culture in the years after his death. A twentieth-century Russian priest, Pavel Florenskii, writes that 'St Sergius understood the azure-blue of the heavens [as the emblem] of the imper-turbable world of eternal and perfect love. He understood that world of love as both the object of contemplation and the commandment to be realized in every life – as the foundation for the building of the Church and the person, of government and society.'[15] St Andrew Rublev seems to have received through the Orthodox faith and through the particular tradition embodied in St Sergius a profound appreciation of the mystery of the Holy Trinity which he was able to express in the famous icon he painted for the cathedral of St Sergius and the Holy Trinity in the period 1408–1425. The icon was com-missioned by the abbot of the monastery who asked Rublev to represent the Holy Trinity as the source and example of all unity.[16]

Rublev's icon of the Trinity is remarkable for what is left out, as well as for what is put into the icon. Gone are the figures of Abraham, Sarah and the servant; gone are the elaborate table details, items of bowls, cutlery and nap-kins; gone, too, is the elaborate architectural setting that was common in many icons of this theme. His icon consists of the three angelic figures seated around three sides of a table on which stands a chalice with the head of a lamb – the image of sacrifice and communion. The form of the angels is incorporated within a circular design, and the form of the two outer angels echoes the form of the central chalice. Sacrificial love and communion seem to permeate the whole composition.

The upper part of the icon has three stylized details: a house, a tree and a mountain peak. All three are so stylized that they must inevitably be seen as having symbolic significance. The house is architecturally impossible; it represents the house of Abraham and Sarah, their dwelling place, but also it moves our attention on to the inner world, the inner dwelling place of God in the human heart, and the mystery of the Church as the sacrament of God's presence. The tree signifies the oak of Mamre, but it also seems to hint at the tree of life, and the new life which is opened up to us through the Incarnation and the revelation of the mystery of the Holy Trinity. The mountain top calls to mind Mount Moriah and Abraham's willingness to sacrifice Isaac, and also the other mountains associated with divine revelation such as Mount Tabor and the Mount of Olives. The mountain peak is bent towards the centre of the icon, towards the circle of the self-giving love of the Trinity, and to the sacrificial symbol at the centre of the group of three seated angels. 'The Lamb slain from the foundation of the world' is the phrase used in Revelation 13:8 (AV), and St Peter speaks of Christ as the 'Lamb without blemish and without spot; who verily was foreordained before the foundation of the world, but was manifest in these last times for you' (1 Peter 1:19 AV). Sacrificial love is at the heart of the Trinity, the source of both the work of creation and the work of redemption and sanctification.

The lowest part of the icon uses a technique sometimes described as inverse perspective to draw us into the icon. In many icons the lines of perspective are different from what is familiar to us. We are used to lines of perspective that meet in the distance, at the back of a picture; this places the final focal point deep in the distance. In icons things are often very different. Inverse perspective involves the lines of perspective meeting not at the back of the scene, but in front of it, out of the icon, in the person who stands before the icon. The reality within the icon is projected forward to the worshipper; revelation is given, and the mystery opened up to us is not the mystery of distance and absence, but the mystery of presence. Here with Rublev's icon of the Holy Trinity, the technique of inverse perspective at the lowest level of the icon is used to raise us into the circle of divine self-giving love. In the upper level of the icon the symbols point us into the communion of love: it is there that we will discover our true dwelling place; there we will find the source of life; there we find true sacrifice and communion.

Inevitably there has been a huge amount of speculation about which of the angelic figures is intended to represent a particular person of the Holy Trinity. Readers must look elsewhere to follow up this particular issue.[17] Suffice it to say that two main schools of thought exist: one suggesting that we should look from our left to right in the order of 'Glory be to the Father, and to the Son, and to the Holy Spirit'; the other school of thought sees the central figure as representing the person of the Father, the one on his right as the Son, and the one on his left as the Holy Spirit. Rublev's genius seems to give space for these two opinions to be cogently argued, while at the same time leaving us an image of the Holy Trinity in its harmony and unity, the contemplation of which gives us the grace to overcome the hateful divisions which we experience within ourselves and beyond us in the world.

> Let us celebrate Pentecost, and the coming of the Spirit, and the appointed day of promise, and the fulfilment of hope, and the mystery which is as great as it is precious. Wherefore unto thee, O Lord, the maker of all things, do we cry: Glory to thee. Glory to the Father, and to the Son, and to the Holy Spirit, now, and for ever, and unto the ages of ages, Amen.[18]

We now turn to the second aspect of the celebration of Pentecost.

> Thou art, of a truth, the Master of all men, O God our Saviour, the hope of all the ends of the earth, and of those who are afar off upon the sea; Who, on this last and great and redeeming day of the Pentecostal feast, didst reveal unto us the mystery of the Holy Trinity, one in Essence, coeternal, undivided and unmingled; and didst pour out the inspiration and descent of the holy and life-giving Spirit, in the form of tongues of fire, upon thy holy apostles; and didst appoint the same to be heralds of the glad tidings of our holy faith; and didst make them confessors and teachers of the true divine knowledge.[19]

This text sums up the significance of the Day of Pentecost. God reveals the mystery of the Holy Trinity. God pours out the inspiration of the Holy and life-giving Spirit upon the apostles. God appoints the apostles as heralds of the faith, and makes them confessors and teachers of true divine knowledge. It is this significance of the Day of Pentecost that is expressed in the icon of the Descent of the Holy Spirit (Plate 5). This icon, like that of the Trinity, is one of harmony and coherence. The apostles are shown seated in a semi-circle in the Upper Room. At the top of the icon the segment of a circle represents the heavenly realm from which rays descend. Tongues of fire are often shown above the heads of the apostles, but not always. The attitudes, posture and gesture of the apostles express a sense of mutual cohesion and communion. St Peter and St Paul face each other at the head of the apostolic group, and this in itself makes us realize that the understanding expressed in the icon is not restricted to the events of the Day of Pentecost itself. St Paul's place in the icon shows a wider concern: the unity and coherence of the whole Church, as the Spirit gives to the Church that gift of unity which is the unity of the Holy Trinity itself, the unity which Christ prayed would be experienced by his disciples and those who believed through their word. The Spirit bestowed at

Pentecost is the Spirit of Truth invoked by the Church as the One who will cleanse us by his indwelling:

> O heavenly King, the Comforter, Spirit of Truth, who art in all places and fillest all things; Treasury of good things and Giver of life: Come, and take up thine abode in us, and cleanse us from every stain: save our souls, O good One.[20]

The apostolic group receives the grace that brings wisdom, the wisdom that enables them to bring the universe into the unity of God's kingdom:

> When thou didst send thy Spirit, O Lord, while the apostles sat, then were the Hebrew children affrighted with dread as they gazed; for they heard them speak to one another in strange tongues, as the Spirit gave them utterance. For though unlearned they were made wise, and bringing the Gentiles unto the faith, proclaimed things divine.[21]

> Blessed art thou, O Christ our God, who hast revealed fishers most wise, sending down upon them the Holy Spirit, and thereby catching the universe as in a net. O Christ our God, who lovest mankind, glory to thee.[22]

> When the Most High confounded the tongues, he dispersed the nations: but when he distributed the tongues of fire, he called all men into unity. Wherefore, with one accord, we glorify the All-holy Spirit.[23]

In the centre of the lower part of the icon stands a royal figure representing or personifying the peoples of the world. He stands against a dark background symbolizing the darkness and ignorance of the world, but in his hands he holds a linen cloth containing twelve scrolls – the apostolic teaching that brings light and hope into the darkness. Through the descent of the Spirit and the apostolic mission of the Church all people are called into the unity of God's kingdom.

This icon, taken together with the Trinity icon, expresses in a profound way the unity and harmony into which humanity is called. From the Trinitarian 'imperturbable world of eternal and perfect love' comes into being the Church within which we can cry, 'Blessed is the kingdom of the Father, and of the Son, and of the Holy Spirit.' From within the community of the Church we enter into the communion of the Holy Trinity from whom we derive our very form and existence. The two icons for the feast of Pentecost together reveal the mystery that is both an 'object of contemplation' and also the 'foundation for the building of the Church and the person, of government and society'.

CELEBRATING THE EASTER MYSTERY

In all the icons we have considered there is a mysterious quality of stillness and calm which takes us out of ourselves. Although the events which are celebrated in these feasts are dramatic and remarkable, their celebration in the icons is marked with a sense of sobriety. Theological truth is being set before us for our contemplation, truth that will find a home in our innermost being as well as in the community of the Church; truth that will transfigure our lives by its grace and power. This truth that is revealed and celebrated sets our lives beyond ourselves. We are called to stand out, to go out from ourselves into the kingdom of the Father and of the Son and of the Holy Spirit.

The Anastasis icon shows Adam being released from the darkness and bondage of Hades and taken by Christ into the light and glory of the risen life. The Ascension icon shows Christ ascending into heaven, with the Mother of God and the apostolic community looking up in worship and faith. The Trinity icon sets before us the mystery that is the source of our being and the goal of our creation – the divine life of the Holy Trinity. The icon of the Descent of the Spirit reveals the harmony and unity of the Church within which by the grace of the Spirit each person is not a separated individual, but finds his or her place in community and in communion.

These icons have a permanent place in Orthodox Churches on the Church feasts tier on the iconostasis, and may also be represented on the vaults of the church roof. On a feast day the appropriate icon is set out on a stand in church to be venerated by the faithful as part of the celebration. The realities represented in the feasts and their icons are not simply part of the temporal sequence of the liturgical life of the Church; they form part of a central reality of revelation and faith that is a continuous, ever-present part of the consciousness of Orthodoxy.

NOTES

1   Isabel Florence Hapgood, *Service Book of the Holy Orthodox-Catholic Apostolic (Greco-Russian) Church* (Boston and New York: Houghton, Mifflin & Company, 1906), p. 226.
2   Evagrius Ponticus, *The Praktikos & Chapters on Prayer*, translated, with an introduction and notes, by John Eudes Bamberger OCSO (Kalamazoo, Michigan: Cistercian Publications, 1981), p. 65.
3   *The Services for Holy Week and Easter Sunday, from the Triodion & Pentecostarion*, pp. 282–3. Greek and English Text (London: Williams & Norgate, 1915), pp. 282–3.
4   *The Lenten Triodion*, translated from the original Greek by Mother Mary and Archimandrite Kallistos Ware (London and Boston: Faber and Faber, 1978), p. 337.
5   *The Services for Holy Week and Easter Sunday*, p. 287.
6   Op. cit., p. 305.
7   *The Philokalia*, translated by G. E. H. Palmer, Philip Sherrard and Kallistos Ware. Volume III (London and Boston: Faber and Faber, 1983), p. 337.
8   N. Orloff, *The Ferial Menaion or the Book of Services for the Twelve Great Festivals and New Year's Day* (London: J. Davy & Sons, 1900), p. 261.
9   Ibid., p. 261.
10 Hapgood, op. cit., p. 243.
11 Ibid., p. 243.
12 Ibid., p. 243.
13 Orloff, op. cit, p. 258.
14 Ibid., p. 255.

Plate 4.   The Holy Trinity: Novgorod School; end of 15th century.
Reproduced by permission of The Temple Gallery.

87

Plate 5.   The Descent of the Holy Spirit: Cretan School; 16th century.
Reproduced by permission of The Temple Gallery.

15 Archpriest Pavel Florenskii, *On the Icon*, translated with an introduction and notes by John Lindsay Opie. 'Eastern Churches Review', Vol. VIII, No. 1, 1976, (Oxford: Clarendon Press), p. 24.
16 Egon Sendler, *The Icon – Image of the Invisible* (California: Oakwood Publications, 1988), p. 104.
17 L. Ouspensky and V. Lossky, *The Meaning of Icons* (Crestwood, New York: St Vladimir's Seminary Press, 1982).
18 Hapgood, op. cit., p. 246.
19 Ibid., p. 255.
20 Ibid., p. 250.
21 Ibid., p. 246.
22 Ibid., p. 247.
23 Ibid., p. 247.

FURTHER READING

J. Baggley, *Doors of Perception – Icons and Their Spiritual Significance* (London: Mowbray, 1987).
L. Ouspensky and V. Lossky, *The Meaning of Icons* (Crestwood, New York: St Vladimir's Seminary Press, 1982).
L. Ouspensky, *The Theology of the Icon* (Crestwood, New York: St Vladimir's Seminary Press, 1992).
M. Quenot, *The Icon, Window on the Kingdom* (London: Mowbray, 1992).
Egon Sendler, SJ, *The Icon – Image of the Invisible* (California: Oakwood Publications, 1988).
R. Temple, *Icons: A Sacred Art* (London: The Temple Gallery, 1989).
R. Temple, *A Brief Illustrated History of Icons* (London: The Temple Gallery, 1992).

Prints of icons can be bought through the St Paul MultiMedia, 199 Kensington High Street, London W8 6BA.

ACKNOWLEDGEMENTS

All biblical quotations except where stated otherwise are from the Revised Standard Version of the Bible.

I am grateful to Richard Temple of the Temple Gallery, London, for providing the photographs of icons referred to in the text.

A BAPTISMAL REMEMBRANCE:
A THANKSGIVING FOR BAPTISM

It is envisaged that those who have been recently baptized will be specially invited to church on a particular Sunday in the Easter season. This short celebration is seen to meet the pastoral need of maintaining contact with baptism families, and is constructed to fit either a eucharistic celebration, or a Service of the Word. It should take place at the font, which might be specially decorated for the occasion, and follow after the sermon. Those especially invited to the service might be asked to bring their baptismal candles. This remembrance of baptism is not modelled on the overworked form for the renewal of baptismal promises, but takes the form of a thanksgiving for the gifts and status bestowed by God at baptism. It is inspired by a sermon preached by Augustine of Hippo to the newly baptized on the Sunday after Easter in which he urges them to return and venerate the font, where their Christian life began, and stands in the tradition of the *Pascha annotinum*, the communal commemoration of baptism, and the baptismal memorials which were celebrated at Vespers in the Octave of Easter and are found in the early liturgical books.

The baptismal memorial takes place after the Gospel, or the sermon, and the following hymn may be sung as the congregation processes to the font:

> Sing out to God, whose clear command
> Turned raging sea to firmest land;
> And led his people on their way
> From Egypt's night to Canaan's day.

> As waters part within the womb
> For fire to leap up from the tomb,
> So at the font the Spirit's flame
> Brands on the newly-born a name.

But waters flow once more to bless
The thirsty in the wilderness;
And from the dying belov'd Son
The streams of resurrection run.

May God the Father, who has raised
Our Saviour Jesus Christ, be praised;
Who in the Spirit we adore
As Trinity for evermore.

(Hilary Greenwood. Tune: NEH 232)

When the people have gathered around the font, which might be especially decorated for the occasion, the minister shall say:

Through baptism we have been adopted as God's sons and daughters, bound to Christ in his death and resurrection, released from the grip of sin and incorporated into his body the Church. As we make this joyful commemoration of baptism, let us ask the Lord that the gifts and promises we have received through our rebirth in water and the Spirit may be fulfilled in our lives and in the lives of those committed to our care, and that persevering in faith and love we may enter into the full inheritance of the saints in the eternal Kingdom of the Father, Son and Holy Spirit.

But first I must ask you, are you resolved to grow in the Spirit of Christ, the fount of wisdom, and for your own lives to be channels of God's love and peace?

By the grace of God, I am.

At this point the baptismal candles may be lit from the Paschal candle, which should be brought in the procession from its usual place in the sanctuary to the font.

Biblical Reading (John 7:37–9):

On the last day of the feast, the great day, Jesus stood up and proclaimed, 'If any one thirst, let him come to me and drink. He who believes in me, as the scripture has said, "Out of his heart shall flow rivers of living water."' Now this he said about the Spirit, which those who believed in him were to receive; for as yet the Spirit had not been given, because Jesus was not yet glorified.

Responsory:

The voice of the Lord is upon the waters.
The voice of the Lord is upon the waters.

The voice of the Lord has declared,
'You are my people.'

Glory to the Father and to the Son and to the Holy Spirit.
The voice of the Lord is upon the waters.

Canticle:

Refrain:

Truly, I tell you, no one can enter the kingdom of God without being born of water and the Spirit.

1   Blessed be the God and Father of our Lord Jesus Christ: By his great mercy we have been reborn as children of God.

2   To a living hope through the resurrection of Jesus Christ from the dead: and to a glorious inheritance that can never spoil.

3   We have come to that cornerstone, in God's sight chosen and precious: to be built as living stones into a spiritual house.

4   For we are a royal priesthood, God's own people: and have tasted the goodness of the Lord.

5   That we may declare the wonderful deeds of him: who has called us out of darkness into his marvellous light. (1 Peter 1:3, 4 and 9)

The refrain is repeated by all:

Glory to the Father and to the Son:
and to the Holy Spirit;
as it was in the beginning, is now:
and shall be for ever. Amen.

Prayer of Thanksgiving:

We give you thanks and praise O gracious God,
that through holy baptism you have welcomed
and received us in your Son. By your Holy Spirit
you restore us in your image, and bestow upon us
the dignity and freedom of the children of God.
Help us to be true to our baptismal promises;
may the Spirit continue the good work begun
in us, that we may follow your ways,
reject what is false and unjust,
and renounce all that corrupts and destroys
your good creation. We ask this in the name
of him in whom all things are being renewed,
Jesus Christ our Lord. Amen.

If this memorial takes place at a celebration of the Eucharist, the services resume at the Peace.

The Peace:

> There is one body and one Spirit, one hope, one faith, one baptism, one God and Father of us all.
> Maintain the unity of the Spirit in the bond of peace.

> The peace of the Lord be always with you.
> **And also with you.**

A selection of suitable Proper Prefaces for the Eucharistic Prayer can be found in Enriching the Christian Year, *pp. 190–1.*[1]

> The Blessing:

> May God, who in Christ humbled himself and was born in human likeness, restore us to reflect the image of his divine glory; and the blessing of the triune God, Father, Son and Holy Spirit, be upon us and remain with us always.
> **Amen.**

> Let us bless the Lord. (Alleluia! Alleluia!).
> **Thanks be to God! (Alleluia! Alleluia!).**

NOTES
1   Perham, M. (SPCK, 1993).

RECEIVING THE BLESSING OF

EASTER: ANOINTING IN CHRIST

. . . The congregation gathers round the newly baptized. The sponsors who have had particular care for each candidate lay hands on them, and take turns to pray, touching as they do so the candidate's eyes, ears, nostrils, mouth, hands. The candidate feels the pressure of each hand and smells the scent of oil, its wetness contrasting with that of the baptismal water:

the eyes: 'May Christ enlighten your eyes to see his glory.'

the ears: 'May Christ open your ears to hear his word.'

the nostrils: 'May Christ enrich your delight in his grace.'

the mouth: 'May Christ inspire you to speak his praise.'

the hands: 'May Christ strengthen you to do his will.' . . .

When people discuss anointing, it is rarely in the kind of context described above. But it is the variety of contexts which make it so powerful. A symbol which is intimate, direct, and which conveys so many meanings is not one to be neglected.

In the New Testament, anointing with olive oil is attested only in the case of the Apostles or church elders anointing the sick (Mark 6:13; James 5:14–15). There is no evidence that anointing was at this stage part of the rites of initiation, but the language of anointing was very common, depending as it does on the consciousness of Jesus as the Christ-Messiah – the Anointed One. Thus Paul says that 'God . . . establishes us with you in Christ, and has anointed (*chrisas*) us, by putting his seal on us and giving us his Spirit in our hearts as a first instalment' (2 Cor. 1:21–2 NRSV). And the first letter of John (2:20) says 'You have been anointed (*chrisma echete*) by the Holy One, and all of you have knowledge.' With the language of the church as the royal priesthood in 1 Peter, evoking the inauguration of the Old Testament kings and priests by anointing and their fulfilment in Jesus of Nazareth, anointing was a symbol waiting to be brought into practice.

These references do not have an immediate reference to initiation, though their relevance is obvious. Over the years their symbolic value has been explored for the most part in initiatory texts and so most of the instances I shall discuss are in that context. But we are moving today into a new style of worship with a particular emphasis on commemoration. The church calendar is being rediscovered, and with it a desire for a fuller and more varied celebration of the events of the Gospel. There is also a higher awareness of commemorating events in our own lives, with the observance of anniversaries. So language which has been applied to one arena is perforce being borrowed for use elsewhere. And the language of sharing in the kingship and high priesthood of Christ, which in the tradition has appeared, if anywhere, in the symbolism of initiation, is liable to be found in the ways in which we celebrate our Christian life through the church's year. The feasts of the Baptism of Christ and of Christ the King are novel in the Western calendar and have yet to achieve a maturity in popular and liturgical spirituality. Both look for their fulfilment to the Easter season, when Jesus was seen as the Risen and ascended Lord and Christ, and, as Paul says, 'was declared to be Son of God with power according to the spirit of holiness by resurrection from the dead' (Rom. 1:4).

To some extent recent scholarship has moved initiation away from a narrow dependence on the spirituality of dying and rising with Christ as seen in Romans 6, and has been drawing on other scriptural explorations of baptism and the Christian life. But this may free some aspects of liturgical spirituality to dwell more closely on the Easter Mystery. Here, every year, and not just once in our baptism, we liturgically enter into the mystery of the anointed Christ and receive his grace. And anointing may be a way of doing just this.

While the evolution of anointing with olive oil was natural and, in Mediterranean society, all but inevitable, it is hardly compulsory or obligatory. (Tattooing seems to have been an early variant.)[1] Britain lies outside that area of civilization delineated by the extent of the olive tree, and we must be conscious that we are not dealing with a substance familiar to everyday use but one which is strange to many. Perhaps the most important development in favour of the practice of anointing is not anything ecclesiastical, whether it be ecumenical or biblical, but the growing consciousness of oils in massage, aromatherapy and the like.[2] Oil is familiar again, and the person who compares anointing to aromatherapy is as correct as the one who recognizes the act of feeding and the equivocal nature of drunkenness in the eucharist, or refreshment, life, and danger in the water of baptism.

Through the first centuries of the Christian Church the nature and symbolism of oil crystallized around three oils: that used in healing; the oil for those preparing for baptism (the oil of catechumens); and the chrism – oil, traditionally scented, used for anointing those just baptized, and candidates at confirmation and ordination. The Roman Catholic Church maintains the three to this day as does the Orthodox Church, and some Anglicans have revived the practice. The usual practice is to make the sign of the cross on the forehead in oil, but there are many traditional variants: the newly baptized have chrism poured on the head (the idea being to leave the forehead for confirmation), priests at their ordination are signed on their hands, the sick likewise for healing (and many other parts of the body as well), and anyone who has witnessed the baptism of a Greek Orthodox child will have noticed the care taken to cover every square inch of the body. At various times in history the symbolic language has been given free rein. In our own day the important thing is to avoid minimalism and, whatever action is made, to make it simply and fully.

The Roman Catholic custom is for the oils to be blessed by a bishop at the Chrism Mass on Maundy Thursday or some other convenient day shortly before Easter. Again this is adopted by many Anglicans, but others, for instance those Evangelicals who have rediscovered anointing from Scripture, have not seen the need of the episcopal link and use what olive oil is to hand.

But where oil is not appropriate, the symbolism of the action of anointing can be communicated in other ways, in particular in the laying-on of hands and/or making the sign of the cross, either with or without any particular substance. (To describe all these without distinction I shall sometimes use the ancient term *sealing*.) The use of ash on Ash Wednesday has a clear and immediate meaning, and from this we should learn a confidence with the symbols we use. We are in a period where we can be inventive and try to discover what symbols carry the same immediacy.

But what does sealing seek to convey? A common denominator, if one can put it that way, is God's blessing. This is the case whether it is in baptism, or confirmation, ordination, healing or reception into a denomination – and anointing has been used in all these cases. The grace of the Holy Spirit has a high priority, though over-emphasis on that aspect has created problems in the understanding of confirmation, and so we might beware of being over-categorical. But one major strand is that in this ceremony the Christian individually *receives*, and the importance of this can hardly be over-emphasized. For our own culture is so much bound up with what we say and do, about self-affirmation and so on (all perfectly good in themselves) that we tend to interpret worship overmuch in those terms. We are less adept at receiving.

As an example of this, at a popular level baptism is understood all too often as being about making our promises to God, rather than as being a sacrament of God's acting on us. When it is interpreted in this way, the 'Renewal of Baptismal Vows' (as it is called in the Church of England's *Lent, Holy Week, Easter*) is a commemoration of the wrong side of baptism. The Roman Catholic rite has a sprinkling of water over the congregation which maintains some reference to the divine action, but in Anglican circles many see the sprinkling as either popish or silly, and simply omit it. But to have a series of vows and no symbol of receiving verges on pelagianism. In this case usually some action with water is most appropriate: where sprinkling seems feeble, perhaps the members of the congregation should come to the font and sign themselves with the sign of the cross using water, or splash water over their own faces – something fuller than the old minimalism. In all rites of baptism, and in rites which are evoking baptism, the stress on receiving needs to be preserved. Confirmation does this with the traditional hand-laying (with or without anointing). Services of healing do the same. In instances where someone is making a solemn act of entering on church life again after lapsing, say after confirmation, then an act of reception by the church might include sealing.

Sealing in initiation

Sealing does not exist in isolation. It functions in relation to its context. In the history of Christian liturgy, the service of baptism very rarely finishes with the immersion. Leaving aside the controversial role of the hand layings in the Acts of the Apostles, we find the *Didache* has a simple immersion without any other ceremonies, and the early Syrian tradition had only a preliminary anointing. But the Western practice, at least from the time of Hippolytus and Tertullian in the late second and early third centuries AD, was to have subsequent rites affirming the immersion. Even among the churches of the Reformation the immersion was not necessarily the conclusion of the rite. In the Church of England the 1552 *Book of Common Prayer* had the signing with the cross on the child's forehead, and the contemporary rite of John à Lasco had a prayer for the child and the whole congregation to be sealed in the gift of regeneration. Among modern Protestant rites the same principle often holds, for example the baptism service in the *Book of Common Order* of the Church of Scotland of 1940 has an individual blessing of each candidate immediately after the immersion and a declaration of reception into the church. Later editions of the baptism of infants supplement this by the Aaronic blessing, said or sung over all the newly baptized together and alter the declaration to apply to all together. But the end result of all these liturgies is to complement and affirm the act of immersion.

In a previous study of the rites of initiation, I have tried to portray the various attendant ceremonies as important not so much in themselves as in their relation to the immersion. Speaking of the liturgies of the ancient church, I said that

> The ceremonies before the immersion were essentially preparatory – they speak of enabling, purification, and communicate the 'negative' aspects of baptism – forgiveness of sins, death to sin the world and the devil; and the ceremonies after the immersion likewise affirm what has taken place by communicating the 'positive' aspects – incorporation into Christ, priesthood and royalty, sanctification, the purity of the Christian life. The ceremonies need to be seen in their relation to the immersion rather than independently of it; they function as a commentary on and extension of the immersion.[3]

If we see the anointing in this light, then we are in no way reducing the importance of the immersion but are, as it were, spelling out its importance. And just as the baptism service begins with language of repentance and turning away from sin and the world so it needs to be concluded with a strong element of affirmation, welcome and incorporation. To a large extent this is already done in the *Alternative Service Book* (ASB: 1980) of the Church of England with the Welcome and the ceremony of the lighted candle, but there is room here for a richer liturgy making the most of the sealing.

In the *ASB* the signing with the cross may happen either after the Decision or immediately after the immersion (the position in the 1662 *Book of Common Prayer*). The text is set out in the former place in the book, and if for no other reason it has become perhaps the most common place. But it also makes good sense: it prevents the old confused idea that the sign of the cross was the essential part of baptism, and it makes a very satisfying conclusion to the Decision. An anointing at this point is then analogous to the ancient and Roman Catholic anointing with the oil of catechumens, and when people have taken up anointing at this point it is generally with the 'oil of catechumens'. (The *ASB* permits the use of anointing at baptism when the candidate is signed with the cross. There is no change of formula: the oil is simply an optional extra and is usually found only in Anglo-Catholic churches when a tiny amount is dabbed on the forehead. The fullness of sacramental symbolism has yet to make its full effect here!)

This however leaves the post-baptismal section comparatively sparse in the ASB rite. At the time of writing we still await the proposals of the Church of England Liturgical Commission for the revised baptismal rite, and, given the general tendency of recent offerings to enrich the *ASB* format, we may expect that something will be included at this point if only as an option.

But what I wish to do now is set out three motifs which recur in these anointings and which may be explored creatively in the long-term future, in sealings both in initiation and also in other contexts.

Three motifs

The first motif we may consider is the *christological* sealing, identifying the Christian with the Risen and exalted Jesus, the Anointed. Obviously the use of oil and anointing is most suitable here. The motif is an ancient one, going back to Scripture, as we have already seen, and is found liturgically in baptismal rites in the West from Hippolytus' *Apostolic Tradition* of c.215 and also in ancient Syrian rites. Hippolytus' rite is simple in the extreme. The candidate on coming up from the font is anointed by a presbyter who says, 'I anoint thee with holy oil in the Name of Jesus Christ.'[4] Over the years the formula expands, but the connection with the Christ is to be found more in contemporary commentaries, and it is in modern rites that this interpretation is to be found most explicitly in the anointing formula itself, such as we see in the Roman Catholic baptism service:

> The God of power and Father of our Lord Jesus Christ
> has freed you from sin
> and brought you to new life
> through water and the Holy Spirit.
> He now anoints you with the chrism of salvation,
> so that, united with his people,
> you may remain for ever a member of Christ
> who is Priest, Prophet and King.
> *Newly baptised*: **Amen.**

In this modern rite the anointing occupies the same position as does the Hippolytan ceremony mentioned above. However to avoid a duplication of anointings, when the candidate is confirmed at the same service this christological anointing is omitted. For a simple, clear liturgy this is obviously a sensible provision. But it is a great pity that the theology of being united and identified with Christ should have been made an optional alternative to the grace of the Holy Spirit.

The *pneumatological* sealing, to give the rite expressing the presence of the Holy Spirit its tediously correct name, is of course the most common strand in the tradition. In the West it became the separate rite of confirmation, which in many modern rites is once again re-united with baptism. Where confirmation remains separate there is no problem in duplicating the language of the Holy Spirit in order to build up a picture of ever-deepening growth in the life of the Spirit who continually gives us new gifts.

Anointing to signify the gift of the Spirit was to be found in Cranmer's 1549 *Book of Common Prayer*, where the immersion finishes with a very full formula accompanying an anointing:

> Almighty God the Father of our Lord Jesus Christ, who hath regenerated thee by water and the Holy Ghost, and hath given unto thee remission of all thy sins: he vouchsafe to anoint thee with the unction of his Holy Spirit, and bring thee to the inheritance of everlasting life.

But we would be rash to read in this any notion of the Spirit being *given* at this very moment by virtue of either the formula or the action. Cranmer was always careful to preserve a distinction between the sign and the thing signified, and this formula is best read as a prayer for the anointing of the Holy Spirit.

In our own day, the Episcopal Church of the United States (ECUSA: *Book of Common Prayer* 1979) and the Anglican Church of Canada (*Book of Alternative Services* 1985) have a version of this prayer which is said in full sight of the congregation after the immersion:

> Heavenly Father,
> we thank you that by water and the Holy Spirit
> you have bestowed upon *these* your *servants*
> the forgiveness of sin,
> and have raised *them* to the new life of grace.
> Sustain *them*, O Lord, in your Holy Spirit.
> Give *them* an inquiring and discerning heart,
> the courage to will and to persevere,
> a spirit to know and to love you,
> and the gift of joy and wonder
> in all your works. **Amen.**

But the details are different in each case: in ECUSA the prayer is followed by the bishop or priest placing a hand on the person's head, marking the sign of the cross on the forehead (with or without chrism), and the formula:

> *N*, you are sealed by the Holy Spirit in Baptism and marked as Christ's own for ever. **Amen.**

Canada has the signing of the cross (with or without chrism) immediately following the immersion, with the following formula:

> I sign you with the cross,
> and mark you as Christ's own for ever.

and then the prayer is said, again in full sight of the congregation, so it may be detached from the signing by a procession into the body of the church and be simply a post-baptismal prayer rather than one accompanying the signing.

The emphases of the two versions are subtly different and need to be teased out. In ECUSA the prayer is followed by the sealing with mention of the Holy Spirit and of belonging to Christ (a nice, if thin, combination of the christological and pneumatological) and so seems to be taken up entirely with these notions. The Canada version has a christological sealing first, but then the prayer stands more on its own. As such it is a rich prayer not for the giving of the Holy Spirit but for the candidate's Christian life within the life of the community. The congregation are not so much witnesses of the sealing (as they are in ECUSA) as the active context of and participants in the candidate's discipleship. this is of course simply a matter of emphasis. All these strands are present in both versions. But I dwell on (and perhaps exaggerate) the differences in order to explore how varied uses of the same prayer can embody different motifs and emphases, and embrace new important dimensions.

The third category of sealing I call simply *symbolic*. This tries to take account of the ways in the Christian tradition in which the sealing has been used to express some appropriation of the grace of God but has conceptualized it in some manner more diffuse than the categories above. Sometimes it may seem confused, as when the *Missale Gothicum* uses language better suited to giving the white baptismal robe than to an anointing:

> I anoint thee with the chrism of holiness, the garment of immortality which our Lord Jesus Christ first received from the Father, that thou mayest bear it entire and spotless before the judgement seat of Christ and live unto all eternity.[5]

But on other occasions the symbolism is potentially more fruitful. What, for example, are we to make of a remark by St Germanus of Paris?

> The infant is nourished with milk: the catechumen is anointed with chrism. Milk is drawn from the mother's breasts: so chrism is consecrated in the bosom of our holy mother in the Church.[6]

Most important perhaps are the symbolic anointings of the senses, of which a modern example is given at the beginning of this chapter. In the ancient sources this ceremony is found at different stages in the initiatory process. When it is found early on, it is often associated with exorcism; but Cyril of Jerusalem, for example, has this as a post-baptismal ceremony and he connects it a christological/pneumatological anointing. In this case the meaning has become one of sanctifying the senses. The setting suggested above moves far away from the traditional notions of anointing. No presiding minister is suggested, no requirement of episcopal prerogative or presbyteral function; simply a number of Christians praying for one whose initiation they have shared in. No doubt the ordained would share in this, but the emphasis is, as it were, on the community, rather than the hierarchy, as possessors of the Spirit of God and the dignity of Christ.

Commemorative anointings

If we are to follow the logic of using symbolic language to commemorate and celebrate the Easter Mystery, what kind of liturgy might we expect? The Renewal of Baptismal Vows as described above has already travelled down this path, when a facet of the initiation rite has been transferred to the context of celebrating Easter rather than, say, the anniversary of one's own baptism. So here we are following the lead of that development. Very often the Renewal of Baptismal Vows is perfectly adequate for this kind of liturgical celebration. But for churches where this is inadequate or inappropriate (perhaps it has already taken place at the feast of the Baptism of Christ, and one can hardly repeat such an event more than once a year) some other rite might be needed to fill the place. An anointing of members of the congregation during the Easter celebration could answer the case, perhaps with words picking up the christological anointing such as:

> May you remain for every one with Christ
> our great high priest and exalted king.

In some churches the feast of Pentecost is celebrated by an anointing of all who wish to receive it. It is done without fuss, but with care and by taking time with each person. The formula used might be such as:

> By this holy anointing and his great love for you,
> may the Lord fill you with the grace of his Holy Spirit.

In either version, at Easter or Pentecoast, the very simplicity of the rite can communicate its intensity. (Again one could hardly perform such a ceremony more than once a year.) There is no need for commentary, for it carries all within itself. Many will, without prompting, connect the anointing with the signing of the cross in ash forty days before Easter. The rite then serves to balance the beginning of the calendrical cycle and to affirm each person in the celebration and their own Christian belonging.

Good liturgical development comes by entering into Scripture and the Christian tradition and bringing out treasures new and old. I have explored the baptismal tradition of anointing and tried to give a picture of how it might be adapted for new contexts of liturgical spirituality. It remains for others to explore this more fully, and by doing so help lead the Church into a fuller celebration and receiving of the grace of the Risen Christ.

NOTES

1 See C. Jones etc. (ed.), *The Study of Liturgy,* 2nd edn, (London: SPCK, 1992), p. 138 and plate 6. J. Daniélou *The Bible and the Liturgy*, pp. 54–69; for a recent discussion see C. Trevett 'Fingers up Noses and Pricking with Needles: Possible Reminiscences of Revelation in Later Montanism', forthcoming in *Vigiliae Christianae*, 1995.

2 Cf. R. Abrams and H. Slim 'The Revival of Oils in Contemporary Culture: Implications for the Sacrament of Anointing', in M. Dudley and G. Rowell (eds.), *The Oil of Gladness*, (London: SPCK, 1993), pp. 169–75. This book provides a full discussion of the history of anointing.

3 'Liturgy and Ceremonial', in B. Spinks and P. Bradshaw (eds.), *Liturgy in Dialogue* (London: 1993), p. 16.

4 E. Whitaker *Documents of the Baptismal Liturgy* (2nd edn) (London: SPCK, 1970), p. 6.

5 Whitaker, *Documents*, p. 162.

6 Whitaker, *Documents*, p. 165.

11

MORNING PRAYER AND PREPARATION FOR COMMUNION: A DOMESTIC OFFICE FOR SUNDAY MORNINGS

Introduction

This Office has been specifically designed to replace Morning Prayer on a Sunday, where the main service of the day is a eucharist. Sunday is, of course, a 'little Easter', the day when we celebrate the Paschal victory of Christ and give thanks to God for his work of recreation. The earliest Christian witness, particularly the resurrection narratives in the gospels of Luke and John, point to a very close link between the resurrection and the eucharist, and for this reason the eucharist has a pre–eminent place in the Church's worship on a Sunday. The connections between Sunday, the resurrection and the eucharist is well summarized in the slogan of those who sought in the middle of this century to establish the Parish Communion as the chief and central Sunday service. The Communion, they said, was 'the Lord's service, for the Lord's people, on the Lord's day'.

The placing of the eucharist as the central Sunday service has undoubtedly been a proper adjustment to the pattern of parochial Sunday worship, and has done much to deepen our appreciation of what it means to be the Church, the Body of Christ in the world today. But every gain brings a loss, and in a climate where going to church invariably means going to communion, it might be that we have lost that sense, so deeply engrained in the *Book of Common Prayer*, of the need to prepare ourselves to participate in the celebration of the holy mysteries. The following Order of Service, which might be used privately in the home, or celebrated corporately in church, has been constructed to address the need for an adequate preparation for Communion, and draws upon more recent study on the theology and forms of daily prayer. This Office, with its focus upon the resurrection, is recommended for use in the Easter season.

CELEBRATING THE EASTER MYSTERY

This season is a particularly appropriate time to enter more deeply and consciously into the eucharistic mystery, the heart of the Church's worship.

THE PREPARATION

O Lord, you open our lips;
and our mouths glorify and praise your name.

Glory to the Father, and to the Son,
and to the Holy Spirit:
as it was in the beginning, is now,
and shall be for ever. Amen.

THE WORD OF GOD

The Morning Psalm: Psalm 63, verses 1–8; (or one of the following: 5:1–8; 92; 113; 143.)

The Morning Psalm might be sung as a responsorial psalm; see NEH 533.

1 O God, you are my God; eagerly I seek you;
   my soul thirsts for you, my flesh faints for you,
   as in a barren and dry land where there is no water;

2 Therefore I have gazed upon you in your holy place,
   that I might behold your power and your glory.

3 For your loving-kindness is better than life itself;
   my lips shall give you praise.

4 So will I bless you as long as I live
   and lift up my hands in your name.

5 My soul is content, as with marrow and fatness,
   and my mouth praise you with joyful lips,

6 When I remember you upon my bed,
   and meditate on you in the night watches.

7 For you have been my helper,
   and under the shadow of your wings I will rejoice.

8 My soul clings to you;
   your right hand holds me fast.

The Morning Collect:

God most holy, you make morning and evening,
and give us darkness and light.
On this day of resurrection may we walk in the path of righteousness
and follow the way of your Son, so that at the last

we may enter the eternal feast in the
glorious splendour of your kingdom;
through Jesus Christ our Lord. **Amen.**

The Proper Psalm: Psalm 116, (or Psalms 23 and 24).

*The Proper Psalm might be read by a solo voice, or together, but medita-
tively, at normal speech rhythm:*

1   I love the Lord,
     because he has heard the voice of my supplication,
     because he has inclined his ear to me
     whenever I called upon him.

2   The cords of death entangled me;
     the grip of the grave took hold of me;
     I came to grief and sorrow.

3   Then I called upon the name of the Lord:
     'O Lord, I pray you, save my life.'

4   Gracious is the Lord and righteous;
     our God is full of compassion.

5   The Lord watches over the innocent;
     I was brought very low and he helped me.

6   Turn again to your rest, O my soul,
     for the Lord has treated you well.

7   For you have rescued my life from death,
     my eyes from tears and my feet from stumbling.

8   I will walk in the presence of the Lord
     in the land of the living.

9   I believed, even when I said,
     'I have been brought very low.'
     In my distress I said, 'No one can be trusted.'

10   How shall I repay the Lord
     for all the good things he has done for me?

11   I will lift up the cup of salvation
     and call upon the name of the Lord.

12   I will fulfil my vows to the Lord
     in the presence of all his people.

13   Precious in the sight of the Lord
     is the death of his servants.

14 O Lord, I am your servant;
    I am your servant and the child of your handmaid;
    you have freed me from my bonds.

15 I will offer you the sacrifice of thanksgiving
    and call upon the name of the Lord.

16 I will fulfil my vows to the Lord
    in the presence of all his people.

17 In the courts of the Lord's house,
    in the midst of you, O Jerusalem.
    Alleluia!

Psalm Collect:

Eternal God, faithful in your tender compassion,
you give us hope for our life here and hereafter
through the victory of your only Son.
When we share his cup of salvation,
revive in us the joy of this everlasting gift.
We ask this in his name. Amen.

(from 'The Book of Alternative Services'
of the Anglican Church of Canada, 1985)

A Biblical Reading:

*One of the following passages would be appropriate: Exodus 16:9–18;
Exodus 24:3–11; Isaiah 25:6–9; Isaiah 55:1–10; I Corinthians 11:26–8;
Luke 14:15–23; John 6:26–40; John 21:4–14.*

A Responsory may be said:

Christ is the bread of heaven, who gives life to the world.
Lord, give us this bread for ever.

Wisdom has mixed her wine and prepared her table.
Christ is the bread of heaven, who gives life to the world.

Glory to the Father, and to the Son, and to the Holy Spirit.
Christ is the bread of heaven, who gives life to the world.

A Canticle (either the *Benedictus*, or *Gloria in Excelsis*)

The *Benedictus*:

Refrain:

**Alleluia! At the dawning of the day the women came to the tomb;
and the angel declared: 'He is not here, he is risen.' Alleluia!**

Blessed be the Lord, the God of Israel,
who has come to his people and set them free.

The Lord has raised up for us a mighty Saviour,
born of the house of his servant David.

Through the holy prophets, God has promised of old
    to save us from our enemies,
      from the hands of all who hate us,

He promised to show mercy to our forebears,
    and to remember his holy covenant.

This was the oath God swore to our father Abraham:
    to set us free from the hands of our enemies,

Free to worship him without fear,
    holy and righteous before him,
      all the days of our life.

And you, child, shall be called the prophet of the Most High,
for you will go before the Lord to prepare his way,

To give his people knowledge of salvation
by the forgiveness of their sins.

In the tender compassion of our God
the dawn from on high shall break upon us,

To shine on those who dwell in darkness and the shadow of death,
and to guide our feet into the way of peace.

**Alleluia! At the dawning of the day the women came to the tomb;
and the angel declared: 'He is not here, he is risen.' Alleluia!**

Or,

Gloria in Excelsis:

Refrain:

    **Alleluia! I will sing of your strength;
    I will celebrate your love in the morning. Alleluia!**

    Glory to God in the highest,
    and peace to God's people on earth.

    Lord God, heavenly King,
    almighty God and Father,
      we worship you, we give you thanks,
      we praise you for your glory.

Lord Jesus Christ, only Son of the Father,
Lord God, Lamb of God,
you take away the sin of the world:
    have mercy upon us.

You are seated at the right hand of the Father:
    receive our prayer.

For you alone are the Holy One,
you alone are the Lord,
you alone are the Most High,
    Jesus Christ,
    with the Holy Spirit,
    in the glory of God the Father. Amen.

Alleluia! I will sing of your strength;
I will celebrate your love in the morning. Alleluia!

THE PRAYERS

Prayer of Preparation:

We are not worthy, O Christ our Risen Lord that you should come under our roof and abide with us, but in your abundant grace you desire to make yourself known to us. O lover of humankind, you ask us to open the doors of our hearts, that you may enter in with your mercy. You welcome those who turn to you and invite sinners to eat and drink with you; for you alone are holy, and forgiving, and even now you give us a foretaste of that heavenly banquet; where with the Father, and the Holy Spirit, you live and reign, now and for ever. Amen.

Trisagion (*said three times*):

O holy God, holy and strong, holy and immortal,
    have mercy upon us.

The Lord's Prayer:

As we prepare to receive the bread of God's kingdom, let us pray as Christ has taught us:

Our Father in heaven . . .

Collect:

Call us, Lord, as you called those disciples
who journeyed to Emmaus to be your companions.
Like them, may our hearts be excited by your love,
    and our minds enlightened by your Word.

As we recognize you in the breaking of bread,
draw us into closer communion with you
    that we may share your life,
blessed Trinity, Father, Son, and Holy Spirit. **Amen.**

The Conclusion:

Christ our Passover has been sacrificed for us;
so let us celebrate the feast!

The Blessing:

May we be nourished by the Bread of Life. **Amen.**

Let us bless the Lord. Alleluia! Alleluia!
Thanks be to God. Alleluia! Alleluia!

12

CHRISTOPHER IRVINE

SPINNING A TALE AND CATCHING A VISION: PREACHING ON THE ASCENSION

A liturgical scholar has suggested that people can be divided between lumpers and splitters,[1] and this is a neat and amusing way of describing not only how people view history, but different ways in which people approach anything at all. There are those on the one hand who are more analytical in their approach; and on the other, those who view things more holistically, who appreciate a thing as it strikes them. It might be said that these two approaches are exemplified in the earliest Christian witness, in the writings of Luke, who set things down in an 'orderly account'; and of John, who through the language of paradox presents an indivisible account of the story of God's salvation. In his historical style of narrative Luke sets out the fate of Jesus in a more episodic fashion. The ascension of Christ, presented as a temporal event, takes place forty days after the resurrection, and the sending of the Spirit upon the disciples ten days later on the feast of Pentecost. By contrast, John holds in closest tension the cross and resurrection, the glorification of Christ and the sending of the Spirit, and views the mystery as a whole. Indeed the words he places on the lips of Jesus encapsulate the whole Christian story: 'I have come from God, and I am going to the Father.'

It is generally agreed that the feast of the Ascension was not established as a distinctive feast until late in the third century, but clearly what was marked by that feast, that the Risen Christ was drawn into the very heart of God, was part of the Christian consciousness from earliest times, and the language of glory and exaltation was used to express this central conviction.

At the time when the New Testament canon was being fixed, positive decisions were obviously made to exclude documents which included stories of the ascension which were crudely literalistic and which graphically described Christ's ascent into heaven and the amazement of the angels as he travelled through heavenly space. This historical fact lends support to those who are wary and genuinely uncertain about what ought to be said in a sermon on the ascension.

Naïve views of a physical ascent as a temporal event are implausible. However, a more holistic approach to the fate of Jesus and the story of Christian salvation not only resonates with the depths of Christian tradition, but also provides the preacher with a more fruitful approach to what is celebrated at the feast of Ascension. So, let us trawl this particular strand and see what it might yield for the preacher.

One might start, not with the picture presented in Acts 1:9, ' . . . as they were looking on, he was lifted up, and a cloud took him out of their sight', which conjures up images of vertical take-off, but the words of a fifth-century Office hymn for the Ascension (EH 141), which rather than pigeon-holing the saving event, holds together the Incarnation, passion, resurrection, exaltation and glorification of Christ. This unitive view asserts that our humanity, taken by Christ in the Incarnation, is now with God. One theological corollary of this is that the Christ is no longer bound, or confined as he was in the days of his earthly ministry, by the categories of time and space. This latter conviction is what drives the apostolic witness of the Church, for the Gospel which is proclaimed to everyone in every place is that all that Jesus offered and brought to those he encountered in his earthly ministry is available to all people in every place and in every age. The Risen Christ commissions the apostles to make disciples of all nations. God's salvation, in other words, opens up like a horseshoe, and extends until the whole of creation is within its embrace. It is of universal significance and application.

But how is this to be communicated in a way which triggers peoples' imagination and claims their hearts and minds? What exactly is to be proclaimed, and how might we live it out? The answer to these questions might be found in an unlikely source, a well-known children's nursery rhyme:

> Pussy cat, pussy cat where have you been?
> I've been up to London to visit the Queen.
> Pussy cat, pussy cat what did you there?
> I frightened a little mouse under the chair!

The implication in this rhyme is that the cat, despite his adventurous excursion, remained preoccupied with the usual cat routines of life, and so failed to glimpse the sight of majestic glory which was the object of his journey. Unlike the cat in this rhyme, who failed to see above the skirting board, Christians are invited at Ascensiontide to raise their sights above their daily preoccupations, to see the whole picture and then to regard everything else in its light. Ascensiontide, with its imagery of the glorified Christ 'seated at the right hand of the throne of the Majesty in heaven' (Hebrews 8:1), summons Christians to raise their sights, to cast off the blinkers of prejudice, and to contemplate the final scene, the full picture of our human flesh borne and presented by Christ to the Father. As Lewis Carroll, who enchanted and intrigued his audience by his spinning of tales and word games, said: 'That's glory for you!'

But what do we mean by glory? This question strikes at the very heart of the mystery of the ascension, and might be answered by the preacher in the words of Irenaeus of Lyons, who said: 'the glory of God is a person fully alive.' In the first instance, we look to Jesus, who in the words of the epistle to the Hebrews, is the pioneer and perfector of our faith. So, our attention must be focused upon Jesus, who opens for humanity a way to God and reveals the object of our earthly journey. An Orthodox theologian speaks of Jesus in terms of a forerunner, who having entered the very heart of the divine Glory, draws us after him into the intimacy of the life of the Trinity. A solemn procession is formed, and a whole cloud of witnesses rises up to follow the vindicated and glorified Christ. The place where this procession is formed, as it were, is the House of God, where people gather for prayer and worship.[2] For if, as the Orthodox say, worship is 'heaven on earth', the occasion when our sights might be raised and in which we enter upon something much bigger than ourselves, then this is a privileged event, a time when we might catch a glimpse of the divine beauty and majestic splendour. Through our worship we enter the beauty of holiness; we are caught up to heaven, and joined to Christ. If we truly enter into this experience, and train our sights on him who is 'flesh of our flesh, bone of our bone', transfigured and glorified, then we ought to see things differently; and seeing things differently, live differently.

The same challenge and demand is presented in the passage which is set as a New Testament reading for Easter Day: 'If you have been raised with Christ, seek the things that are above . . .' (Colossians 3:1). This cannot be an escape from earthly responsibilities and obligations, but a reordering and sharpening of them. For if the Christian's attention is focused upon Christ, who came not to 'condemn the world, but to save the world' (John 3:17), then he, or she, will come to see his glory reflected back upon the world which is the object of God's love.

There is a slight reprimand in Luke's account of the Ascension: 'Men of Galilee, why do you stand looking into heaven?' and perhaps it is not totally inadmissible to suggest that the sense of these words is that we are not to stare absently into an empty sky to look out for those glimpses of glory which reflect the divine majesty and refract God's splendour. We must look to Jesus, in other words, so that like the Celtic saints, we too might see the natural world of sea, rock and earth as being redolent with divine glory, and recognize Christ in the faces of friends and strangers. All this, and of course much more, is caught by that Old Testament text, which early in the history of Christian liturgy was appropriated as a key text for the feast of the Ascension, namely Psalm 73, verse 24: 'You will guide me by your counsel, and afterwards receive me with glory.'

NOTES

1   P. Bradshaw, *The Search for the Origins of Christian Worship* (London: SPCK, 1992).
2   B. Bobrinskoy, 'Worship and the Ascension of Christ', *Studia Liturgica* 2.2, 113, 1962.

13

A PENTECOST VIGIL

Introduction

The Vigil is essentially a night service of reflection and prayer, and might well culminate in a celebration of the eucharist or the order of Morning Prayer and preparation for Communion which is provided in this book. It is envisaged that the Vigil would take place during the night of the Saturday before Whitsunday. The service itself might well take place in a part of the building which will not be used for the eucharist. In this case the Paschal candle should be placed next to an ambo, or lecturn, so as to provide the visual focus as the Christian community gathers to rehearse its stories, to pray, and to rekindle its hope. A variety of readings are provided and a selection may be made according to the available time. It is recommended that there should be a minimum of four readings. At the entrance of the ministers the Bible may be carried in procession, preceded by the Paschal candle. Each reading has its own psalm and collect-like prayer, and the reflective character of the service would be heightened by the use of deliberate and measured silences between the readings and the psalmody and collects.

The president greets the people and then introduces the Vigil using these or other suitable words:

The light and peace of the Risen Christ be with you all.
And also with you.

Dear friends in Christ, for fifty days we have celebrated the victory of our Lord over sin and death, and made alleluia our song. Now as our easter celebration draws close to its joyful fulfilment, and we complete our season of praise with the appointed day of promise, when God will renew and refresh the face of the earth, let us attend to the story of God's saving help, and prepare our hearts and minds to receive the graces of the Holy Spirit. But first we must pray that as we await the outpouring of the Spirit we may truly hear God's Word, that his truth may find a home in us, and that through the power of the Spirit, our speech and actions may tell of his marvellous work in drawing all humanity into the unity of the kingdom of the Father, the Son, and the Holy Spirit.

As the Bible is placed on the lectern, this prayer may be said:

Eternal God,
we thank you for the gift of your holy Word.
May it be a lantern to our feet,
a light to our path,
as we seek to walk with Christ in his risen life,
in the power of the Spirit,
and to your honour and glory. **Amen.**

A selection from the following readings or other suitable passages of the Old Testament may be used:

Reading: Exodus 19:1–9 and 16–19.

Psalm 81.

This response may be used:

O sing joyfully to the Lord; keep faith, and walk in his ways.

Collect:

God our redeemer,
you are clothed in mystery
yet desire our well-being
and sustain us in our earthly pilgrimage.
As we approach you in our festal celebration
may we grow in holiness,
and make known your name in all the world,
through Jesus Christ, our Lord. **Amen.**

Reading: Numbers 11:16–17, and 24–9.

Psalm 99:

This response may be used:

The Lord reigns in justice, and holy is his name.

Collect:

Holy God,
you call and empower your ministers
to guide the perplexed and relieve their burdens.
Pour upon us your Spirit,
that we may declare your word

and make your purpose known;
for the honour of your name,
and the advance of your kingdom.
We ask this in the name of Christ,
our great High Priest. **Amen.**

Reading: Deuteronomy 31:24–9.

Psalm 130:

This response may be used:

> **O Israel, trust in the Lord, for in him is mercy and forgiveness.**

Collect:

> Ever faithful God,
> Shower your mercy upon us,
> making gentle our stubborn wills;
> that we who have perverted your justice,
> and trusted our own inventions
> may find in you a new beginning
> in the strengthening of the Spirit,
> through Christ our Lord. **Amen.**

Reading: Isaiah 4:2–end.

Psalm 125:

This response may be used:

> **O people of God, be true to the Lord, and seek his goodness.**

Collect:

> God our guide and protector,
> as you come among us
> purge all that is impure and dishonourable,
> and grant us the fruits of the Spirit,
> growing to maturity in our lives;
> through Christ, the true vine,
> and the olive branch of peace. **Amen.**

Reading: Baruch 3:9–23.

Psalm 19:1–11:

This response may be used:

> **Your wisdom, O God, pervades the whole of the world.**

Collect:

Stir us, Creator God,
from the lethargy of sin:
May we seek your ways,
  and follow them,
acting with gentleness and goodness,
and strong in the strength of the Spirit;
through him who is the wisdom and power of God,
Jesus Christ our Lord. **Amen.**

Reading: Ezekiel 36:24–8.

Psalm 51:1–13:

This response may be used:

Create in me a pure heart, O God, and place a steadfast spirit within me.

Collect:

Merciful God,
through the cleansing waters of baptism
you have given us the name of Christians.
By your searching Spirit
remove our hardness of heart,
and implant in us
such repentance and love,
that others may see
what you have called us to be, and give you the glory,
through Christ our Lord. **Amen.**

Reading: Ezekiel 37:1–14.

Psalm 126:

This response may be used:

Revive your people, O God, as we recall your mighty acts.

Collect:

God, the source of all life,
you alone make rivers to flow in the desert place;
summon the spirit of life upon those who are displaced
and who suffer a living death;
that those in despair may find hope,
and the laughter of life may resound in all the world,
adding to the harvest of praise,
in and through Christ, our redeemer. **Amen.**

Reading: Jeremiah 31:31–4.

Psalm 139:1–11:

This response may be used:

Refashion my heart, O God, for you have made me for yourself.

Collect:

Ever faithful and forgiving God,
you are nearer to us than the air we breathe.
Give us the mind of Christ,
that with discerning hearts
we may seek to act with integrity,
and so make your presence felt and known,
now and always. **Amen.**

If the Vigil leads into a celebration of the eucharist, it is suggested that the 'Gloria in Excelsis' is sung at this point. One of the collects set for the day should be said or sung after the 'Gloria'. It is suggested that Romans 8:14–17 is used for the New Testament reading, leaving the traditional reading from Acts (2:1–22) for the main morning celebration. Further appropriate prayers, Proper Prefaces, blessings and dismissal for the Day of Pentecost, the culmination of the Easter season, can be found in Michael Perham's 'Enriching the Christian Year'.[1]

NOTES
1 London, SPCK, 1993.

14

AN INTRODUCTORY RITE FOR THE FEAST OF PENTECOST

This simple rite is intended for the main celebration on Whitsunday. It is envisaged that the whole congregation will join the procession around the church, and Pentecost banners may be carried to add a greater festive air. The church might also be decorated with freshly cut foliage and a profusion of flowers. Small branches of may and lilac might also be carried in the procession representing the burgeoning of nature in the late spring, and reminding the congregation of God's renewal of creation by the operation of the Holy Spirit, the giver of life.

The congregation assembles in the chancel, and the ministers and servers informally enter the sanctuary. The Officiant greets the people with these, or similar words:

>The grace and peace of the Lord through whom all things were made, of God our Creator, and the Holy Spirit, the giver of life be with you all.
>
>**And also with you.**

Introductory Sentence (Luke 24:49):

>Jesus said: stay together until you are clothed with power from on high.

All kneel and pray together in silence.

The Officiant then intones the 'Veni, Creator Spiritus', and the congregation joins in singing this hymn unaccompanied (NEH 348). The Taizé chant 'Veni, Creator Spiritus' might be sung as an alternative to the hymn.

After the hymn the Officiant says:

Come, Holy Spirit of God!
And kindle in our hearts the fire of your love.

The Collect for Purity:

> **Almighty God,**
> **to whom all hearts are open,**
> **all desires known,**
> **and from whom no secrets are hidden:**
> **cleanse the thoughts of our hearts**
> **by the inspiration of your Holy Spirit,**
> **that we may perfectly love you,**
> **and worthily magnify your holy name;**
> **through Christ our Lord. Amen.**

Either A, or B.

A. The Penitential Kyries:

> Lord, you convict the world of sin, and convince it of righteousness. Lord, have mercy.
> **Lord, have mercy.**

> Lord, you reconcile us to yourself and make us one by your Spirit. Christ, have mercy.
> **Christ, have mercy.**

> Lord, you enlighten our hearts and minds, and lead us in the way of truth. Lord, have mercy.
> **Lord, have mercy.**

B. The asperges, or sprinkling with water.

The water being used for the sprinkling may be blessed with the following prayer:

> Eternal God,
> we praise and thank you for your creative love and redemptive power.
> At the dawn of creation your Spirit
> brought order and beauty out of the waters of chaos.
> As your people journeyed through the desert
> you satisfied their thirst with water from the rock.
> To the Samaritan woman, your Son promised the gift
> of water welling up to eternal life.
> Bless this water, + that we may recall our baptismal hope.
> Revive us with the dew of your mercy,
> and bring us to drink of your Spirit,
> through Christ, now risen and glorified. **Amen.**

CELEBRATING THE EASTER MYSTERY

As the congregation are sprinkled with holy water, the following anthem may be sung:

> To the thirsty I will give water without price
> from the fountain of the water of the well of life.
>
> *(Revelation 21:6)*

The Absolution is then given, and all stand for the Processional hymn.

Before the Processional hymn the Officiant may say:

> Let us go forth in peace.
> **In the name of Christ. Amen.**

During the Processional hymn (EH630, NEH142, or some other suitable hymn), the congregation processes around the church and take their usual places in the nave during the penultimate verse.

The eucharist resumes with the 'Gloria in Excelsis', with the clergy and servers in their usual places.

15

A CHRISTIAN SHABBAT MEAL:
A LITURGY FOR THE HOME

The following domestic liturgy, written for use in the home, is based upon and inspired by the Jewish Shabbat ceremonies which are performed each Friday evening at the beginning of the family meal. Certain Jewish customs are retained, such as the central role of women at the celebration, but the forms have been Christianized, and are intended for use on a Saturday evening when a family gathers with friends for an evening meal. This form could also be used by a house-group which has come together to share a meal at the end of the week. One set place at the table should be kept free. This is to provide a symbolic space to welcome Christ, who comes as the stranger, the unexpected guest, as he came to join the disciples at table at Emmaus.

This domestic liturgy has three component parts; the lighting of the evening lamps (for which a large five, or seven branch candle holder might be used); the blessing and setting aside of bread (for which matzo bread might be used); and the blessing and setting aside of wine.

The lighting of the lamps

When the family and guests have gathered around the table the woman of the household says the following prayer:

> As I kindle this light in your honour, O God,
> keep us in your light as children of the day.
> Dispel all grief and sorrow,
> bestow upon us and all who share this table
> the fullness of life, and keep us and our homes
> in your peace and joy;
> for when Christ, who is our life shall appear,
> we shall appear with him in glory.

As the woman lights the candles she says:

Let your face shine upon us, our mothers and our children, O Lord,
and bring us all to the feast of light in the perfect day.

(Other women and children might be invited to light candles at this point)

Turning towards the door, the woman may say:

Let us prepare to meet the bridegroom;
and welcome together the Lord of life.

The blessing and setting aside of bread

After a moment's silence the man of the household takes the bread into his hands, and prays:

Blessed are you, ruler of the universe,
you provide for our needs,
and satisfy us with bread.
May we hunger to see your justice,
and share what you have given us with glad and generous hearts;
that we may be united in your love,
and come to taste your heavenly banquet,
Father, Son and Holy Spirit.

Blessed be God for ever!

At the setting aside of a portion of the bread, the man says:

**Blessed is he who comes in the name of the Lord!
We will bless you in the house of the Lord.**

The blessing of the wine, and the setting aside of a cup

Raising the decanter of wine, the man prays:

Blessed are you, Lord our God,
for your Christ drank the bitter cup of suffering,
and endured the judgement of the nations.
May we receive the vintage of your forgiveness,
    the fruits of his passion,
and come to raise the cup of salvation
with a sacrifice of thanksgiving on our lips,
to the Father, Son and Holy Spirit.

Blessed be God for ever!

At the setting aside of a cup of wine, the man says:

> The Spirit came from heaven like a mighty wind.
> Fill us with the new wine of the Gospel.

A general grace may now be said, and the meal commences.

IMAGES FOR ALL-AGE LEARNING AND WORSHIP

This chapter on images for all-age learning and worship is structured in two parts. The first part discusses basic principles behind all-age learning and worship. The second part sets these principles to work in providing examples of eight specific themes for all-age learning and worship appropriate for the Easter season between Easter Sunday and Pentecost.

All-age participation

Churches of all denominations have become increasingly aware of the importance of all-age learning and worship. As long ago as 1976, the British Council of Churches' report, *The Child in the Church*, emphasized the place of the child alongside adult churchgoers. More recently, the Church of England report, *Children in the Way*, published in 1988, emphasized the view of the shared pilgrimage in the church, where children and adults travel side by side, each learning from the other.

At its best, all-age learning and worship recognizes that church services need to be responsive to the range of individuals present throughout the whole service. This is quite different from the adult services which make concessions to children by telling them a story or withdrawing them for the most boring parts.

All-age learning and worship recognizes that all individual worshippers, adults and children alike, come with different experiences, different needs and different ways of expressing themselves. All-age learning and worship needs to take these differences seriously.

All-age learning and worship also recognizes that individual members of the church can learn best from each other. Learning is a two-way process: children learn from adults and adults learn from children. They are travelling together as a shared pilgrimage and are able to enrich and resource each other for the journey.

There are many occasions in worship where adults and children properly share together. Because individuals differ so greatly there are times, however, when this learning can best take place in sub-groups able to focus on specialist needs.

The programme for the Easter season offered in this chapter assumes a service in which adults and children share; it also assumes opportunities for both to learn separately. Integration is achieved by offering adults and children the opportunity to explore a common theme at their own level and then to share with each other the findings of their exploration.

Easter season

The aim of this chapter is to suggest eight themes for all-age worship and learning to span the Sundays of the Easter season from Easter Sunday to Pentecost. Some churches may wish to provide all-age learning and worship on each of these Sundays and follow the whole sequence of themes. Others may wish to hold only a couple of such services during the eigh-week period and select accordingly. The themes are not tightly anchored to the specified Sundays.

The themes for the eight-week period are clearly suggested by the gospel narratives of the Easter event and the resurrection appearances. The suggested sequence of biblical material is this. Easter Sunday itself uses John's account of Mary coming to the empty tomb (John 20:1–18). Easter 1 draws on John's account of Jesus' appearance to the disciples as they were gathered together behind locked doors (John 20:19–29). Easter 2 draws on the story of the journey to Emmaus (Luke 24:13–35). Easter 3 draws on the narrative of Jesus' appearance by the lakeside (John 21:1–14). Easter 4 draws on the encounter between Jesus and Peter as Jesus asks Peter three times 'Do you love me?' (John 21:15–22). Easter 5 returns to the narrative of the day of the resurrection and draws on Mark's account which emphasizes Jesus going ahead of his disciples (Mark 16:1–8). The Sunday after the Ascension employs the brief account of the ascension in Luke's Gospel (Luke 24:45–53). Finally, Pentecost draws on the narrative from the Acts of the Apostles describing the coming of the Holy Spirit (Acts 2:1–11).

Ways are then suggested to enable adults and children to explore these passages of Scripture at their own level and to share with each other their exploration. The key to this is held in the idea of concrete images.

Concrete images

This suggested programme of all-age learning and worship believes that it is possible to identify a simple and basic concrete image at the core of each of the eight biblical themes. This chapter discusses each theme in turn. Each section begins by unwrapping the biblical narrative to reveal the fundamental concrete image which underpins the narrative. Then it suggests ways in which children and adults can explore the concrete image at their own level and, through such exploration, gain insights into the lectionary theme. Such a strategy is developed from distinctive perspectives on religious language and on the educational process.

Religious language has its roots in concrete, everyday experiences, which are then qualified to enable us to speak about religious realities we are not able totally to grasp. By identifying the concrete image at the core of each biblical narrative, it is possible to enable both adults and children to qualify and develop this image to a level consistent with their own religious maturity.

The concrete images underpinning religious language provide a crucial aid not only for children but for adults as well. After all, religious language is not meaningful until we have grasped the basis from which it is derived. In some cases the concrete image and the religious significance is already closely related in the language of the Scriptures themselves. A good example of this is provided by the image identified for Pentecost, namely *the wind*. Both the Hebrew language of the Old Testament and the Greek language of the New Testament employ the one word for *wind* and for *spirit*. The wind is an essential concrete image underlying our understanding of God the Holy Spirit. The more we experience and think about the wind, the more we can understand and interpret our experience of God the Holy Spirit.

The eight concrete themes explored in this chapter are spring, butterflies, bread, fish, repair shop, journey, crowns and wind. The precise linkage is made explicit in each section.

Project learning

The educational principle on which this programme of all-age learning and worship is based is that of project learning. Language acquires its significance from being grounded in human experience. Project learning structures the opportunities for adults and children to experience the concrete images underpinning religious language. Adults and children are encouraged to explore these images at their own level and at their own pace. The fruit of such explorations are then to be shared.

How project learning takes place will vary greatly from one local church to another, depending on the resources, time and skills available. For example, some churches make no separate provision for children and have neither the space nor the leadership to do so. Some churches operate special children's groups throughout part of the service every week. Some churches operate special children's groups parallel with the whole of the Sunday service one week and then integrate the children into the whole of the service another week. Some churches operate children's groups on a Saturday or weekday evening and then try to link these groups with the Sunday service. The ideas suggested in the chapter need to be adapted differently to suit each local situation.

Exploring the themes

In the second part of the chapter each of the eight themes is explored in turn. Six steps are involved in exploring each theme.

Step One examines the biblical narrative from one focused perspective, highlighting the relevance of the concrete image with which it is associated. For this reason no attempt is made to offer an exhaustive exegesis of the passage. The intention is to highlight the one perspective.

Step Two provides a context for the concrete image and discusses more fully how this relates to the biblical narrative.

Step Three clearly specifies three items for each topic, showing a progression from the concrete image to the religious significance.

Step Four suggests how the concrete image can be explored with children. In each case three types of ideas are presented. The section begins by suggesting an activity which will attract the children's attentions and fire their imagination. Then suggestions are made to translate the image into a display in the church. Finally a suggestion is made for exploring the image through dance or drama which can be shared during the service.

Step Five suggests how the concrete image can be explored with adults. The key here is to make the theme known to the regular members of the congregation the week before so that they can think about the image and make some preparation in advance of coming to the service. It is, of course, recognized that some churchgoers will welcome this more than others. Some will make good use of the opportunity, while others will choose to do nothing about it.

Step Six summarizes the main teaching point to result from the learning process among children and adults.

Working with children

The project learning with children can take place in a number of different contexts and over a varying period of time. The ideal envisaged by this programme is the church which is able to work with children for an hour or an hour and a half on a weekday evening after school or on a Saturday morning. Such a context will allow a range of activities to be explored and a good display to be in place in church for the Sunday service.

Churches where the children are withdrawn for part of the Sunday service will be able to explore each theme in less detail and have less opportunity to display the children's work within the church. Nevertheless, a great deal can be achieved within thirty minutes or so, provided each session is clearly thought through and structured beforehand.

Where there is a close relationship between parents, children and church, some parents might like to develop the project theme at home with their children in advance of the service. The children can then bring their materials with them to the Sunday service to display in church.

Working with adults

The project learning with adults can involve the structuring of home groups which work on the theme before the Sunday service. Whether or not supported by home groups, the suggestion is made that the Sunday theme should be made well known in advance, including both the passage of Scripture and the concrete theme. Some of the worshippers, at least, will then have had the opportunity to think about the theme of the service in advance and to bring something to the service which they can share with the other members of the congregation.

Congregations which prefer a less formal mode of learning will be able to make full use of buzz groups and discussion. For local situations in which this does not appear so appropriate, the same set of ideas can be explored through more formal ways of teaching and preaching.

Spring (Easter Sunday)

Scripture: Read John 20:1–18

John tells the story of the first Easter Sunday with less drama than Matthew. Mary Magdalene, Peter and the other disciple (usually thought to be John) find the empty tomb. John saw the empty tomb and believed. Mary does not understand until she sees the Risen Lord and he addresses her by name. For both John and Mary, their different Eastertide experiences open for them the experience of sharing in the new life of the resurrection.

Image

In pre-Christian times the word 'Easter' itself was associated with the goddess of the spring and the rebirth of the natural world after the death and barrenness of the winter months. In John's account of the first Easter Sunday, the emphasis is on both the reality of the resurrection of Christ and the transforming effect of the resurrection on the lives of those who *experienced* the resurrection. We can begin to appreciate the significance of the gospel's teaching about the resurrection of Christ by exploring our own experiences of new life during springtime.

Aims

The aims of this session are to:

- build on our experiences of spring;
- understand spring as a season of new life;
- see Easter as new life for the people of God.

Children

Go out for a walk. Look for the signs of spring; listen to the sounds of spring; sniff the smells of spring; touch the newly sprouting grass or buds. Look for signs of new life. Alternatively, bring into the room some signs of spring. Display spring flowers or spring buds, play a recording of bird song; assemble pictures of spring.

Draw out the ideas of:

- birds building nests and laying eggs;
- grass growing through cracks in the paving stones;
- new life in the ponds;
- frog spawn and tadpoles;
- buds opening on trees;
- hibernating animals waking;
- lambs being born;
- rabbits in the fields;
- grass growing in the park.

Invite the children to make a display about spring in the church. For example, collect moss, twigs and flowers to make an Easter garden. Decorate eggs as a sign of Easter. Grow cress seeds in an empty egg shell, germinate seeds on blotting paper. Make Easter cards showing symbols of spring and new life. Produce a collage of a spring walk.

Devise a dance or a drama presentation to explore the experiences of a hibernating animal waking up in spring and discovering the experience of 'new life'. The dance or drama can be shared in the service after the gospel reading.

Adults

Invite members of the congregation to bring something to the service which speaks to them of the spring. This may include spring flowers, budding branches, photographs of spring scenes, pictures of spring clipped from magazines, recorded music, or even a spring hat. After the gospel reading invite them to discuss what they have brought in small buzz groups. Or during the peace invite them to find someone who brought something quite similar.

A range of ideas can be developed in discussion, teaching or preaching, including:

- our experience of spring in the past;
- our experience of spring this year;
- images of springtime promoted by the media;
- how springtime can affect our feelings and attitudes;
- how spring is an image for Easter;
- how the resurrection of Jesus promises new life, like spring;
- how we can share with others the excitement of the resurrection.

Teaching point

In the spring we see how life is renewed. Today Jesus' resurrection from the dead brings new life to the people of God.

Butterflies (1st Sunday after Easter)
Scripture: Read John 20:19–29

John describes the power of the Risen Christ to bring about change in the lives of the early disciples. On the first day of the week they were full of fear and hiding behind locked doors because they were afraid of the Jewish authorities who had secured the death of Jesus. In the midst of their fear Jesus comes to the disciples, proclaims peace to them and changes their fear into joy. A week later Jesus comes again. Now he changes Thomas' doubt into faith.

Image

A key idea behind the narratives of the disciples locked behind closed doors is the power of the resurrection to bring about change. Jesus changes the disciples' fear into joy. Jesus changes Thomas' doubt into faith. We can begin to appreciate the significance of the gospel's teaching about the power of the Risen Christ to bring about change in the lives of his followers by exploring our own understanding of the change that takes place in the life of the caterpillar and butterfly.

Aims

The aims of this session are to:

- build on our experiences of caterpillars and butterflies;

- understand the caterpillar and butterfly as a symbol of change and transformation;
- see the resurrection of Jesus as the source and power for change and transformation.

Children

Bring pictures of caterpillars and butterflies, their eggs, larvae and pupae. Make an attractive display of these pictures. Try to create one large butterfly from coloured paper to catch the children's attention as they walk into the room. You may choose to play some music evocative of the flight of butterflies.

Draw out ideas of:

- the butterfly lays eggs;
- the caterpillar comes from the tiny egg;
- the caterpillar eats and grows;
- the caterpillar changes into a chrysalis;
- the butterfly takes shape inside the chrysalis;
- the butterfly emerges;
- the butterfly flies away to freedom;
- the butterfly lays tiny eggs.

Invite the children to make a display about butterflies in the church. For example, design a large collage of butterflies in a colourful garden. Draw a diagram showing the life cycle of the butterfly. Make small colourful butterfly brooches. Make mobiles of butterflies using bright tissue paper to hang in the church. Choose a place for the mobiles where there is a draught so that they move around freely.

Devise a dance or a drama presentation to explore the life cycle of the butterfly. Give special attention to the movement of flight and the feeling of freedom. The dance or drama can be shared in the service after the gospel reading.

Adults

Invite members of the congregation to bring a butterfly to church with them. Some may choose to clip a picture from a magazine. Some may wish to sketch or paint a picture of a butterfly. Some may wish to make a mobile or a brooch. Display them prominently in the church. After the gospel reading invite them to discuss what they have brought in small buzz groups. Or during the peace take time to walk round the church to look at the different butterflies.

A range of ideas can be developed in discussion, teaching or preaching, including:

- our experiences of butterflies;
- occasions when butterflies have created an impression on us;

- how we felt about making a butterfly to bring to church;
- the feelings and images butterflies generate in us;
- why the butterfly is a symbol of change and transformation;
- how Jesus changed the disciples' fear into joy;
- how Jesus changed Thomas' doubt into faith.

Teaching point

The life cycle of the butterfly illustrates how change occurs in the natural world. Jesus' resurrection brings about a profound change in the lives of his disciples. He changes their fear into joy. He changes their doubt into faith.

Bread (2nd Sunday after Easter)

Scripture: Read Luke 24: 13–35

The resurrection appearance on the Emmaus road is related only by Luke. This account is like an early Christian eucharist. Ministry of the Word is followed by ministry of the sacrament. On the journey the disciples studied the Scriptures and began to fit parts of the jigsaw together. However, it was not until the bread was broken that the Risen Christ was fully recognized. Here Jesus clearly performs the fourfold eucharistic action. He took the bread; he said the blessing; he broke the bread; he gave the bread to them. This feast at Emmaus both re-enacted the Last Supper and looked forward to the great wedding supper of the Lamb.

Image

The key idea behind the narrative of the Emmaus road concerns the power of the eucharistic loaf to represent the presence of Christ among the people of God. It is through the breaking of bread that Christ's presence is made known. We can begin to enter the disciples' experience of encountering the Risen Christ in the breaking of bread by exploring our own experiences of bread.

Aims

The aims of this session are to:

- build on our experiences of bread;
- understand the importance of bread in the Christian community;
- see the breaking of bread as the sacrament through which the Risen Christ makes his presence known.

Children

Bring a range of different kinds of bread, in different shapes, sizes, types and colours: white, brown, granary, wholemeal, sliced, matzos, chapatti and so on. If this is not possible, try to gather pictures of different types of bread. Cook a pre-prepared loaf or reheat a loaf to fill the room with the smell of bread. Perhaps it may be possible to find a picture of a baker at work.

Draw out the ideas of:

- how bread is made;
- the flour, yeast, dough, oven, etc. used in making bread;
- how bread is dependent on 'the fruits of the earth';
- how bread is dependent on 'the work of human hands';
- the smell of newly baked bread;
- how different types of bread vary;
- the different ways in which bread is eaten;
- times when you have particularly enjoyed bread;
- how bread is a basic food.

Invite the children to make a display about bread in the church. For example, design a collage showing different types of bread. Design a flow chart showing how bread is made, beginning from sowing the corn. Make an advert promoting bread. Make a list of the different ways bread is eaten, including all different sandwich fillings. Bake bread, some of which can be used for the eucharist and some which can be shared with the congregation during or after the service.

Devise a dance or a drama presentation about bread in the making. One child, or a group of children, is the cook. Other children represent the range of ingredients. The ingredients are gradually added and mixed together. The mixture is put into the area where it rises and overflows the tin. The dance or drama can be shared at the service after the gospel reading.

Adults

Invite members of the congregation to bring to the service something which speaks to them of bread. This may include a baking tin, a recipe, a wrapping from a loaf of bread, an advertisement for bread, a picture, a poem, or a text from Scripture. Before the gospel reading invite them to discuss what they have brought in small buzz groups. During the Peace invite them to organize what they have brought in display areas.

A range of ideas can be developed in discussion, teaching or preaching, including:

- our experiences of eating fresh bread;
- our experiences of eating different types of bread in different places;
- images of bread throughout the world;
- different brands available locally;
- the experience of the disciples on the Emmaus road;
- our experiences of sharing bread in the eucharist;
- how different churches share the eucharistic bread;
- our meeting with the Risen Christ in the breaking of bread.

Teaching point

The loaf of bread stands right at the centre of Christian worship. When Jesus broke bread at Emmaus his disciples recognized his presence with them. We, too, come to recognize Jesus' presence at the eucharist.

Fish (3rd Sunday after Easter)
Scripture: Read John 21:1–14

After the crucifixion, some of the disciples appear to have returned to their work as fishermen. Simon Peter, Thomas, Nathaniel, James and John and two other disciples had been fishing all night and yet caught nothing. In the first light of morning Jesus joins them on the shore. They recognize Jesus only after they have landed a large catch, following his advice. Jesus then invites them to share breakfast with him and hosts a fellowship meal.

Image

This narrative of the resurrection appearance by the lakeside had a great influence on early Christian art, where the eucharist was pictured as a meal presided over by Christ, with fish and bread on the table. The fish also became a key secret sign in the early Church, whereby Christians could recognize each other in times of persecution. The Greek word for fish, ICHTHUS, makes up the initial letters for 'Jesus Christ, God's Son, Saviour'. We can begin to enter into the disciples' experience of meeting and feasting with the Risen Christ at the lakeside by drawing on our own experiences of fish and fishing.

Aims

The aims of this session are to:

- build on our experience of fish;
- understand the fish as a Christian symbol;
- link the lakeside appearance of the Risen Christ with the eucharist.

Children

Create the atmosphere of a fishing scene. Display posters or pictures clipped from magazines showing anglers by the river bank, small fishing boats in harbour, deep-sea fishing boats. Display model boats, or fishing nets, or a fishing rod. Talk about who has been fishing and what it is like.

Draw out the ideas of:

- different types of fishing;
- fishing boats and trawler nets;
- angling and fishing rods;
- people who fish for fun;
- people who earn their living by fishing;
- different types of fish;
- fish as a rich food resource;
- different ways of cooking fish.

Invite the children to make a display about fish and fishing. For example display a net through part of the church and make fish to suspend in the net. Make fish and suspend them as mobiles. Make a model of the shore, with boats, fish and fishermen. Design a collage of a fishing scene. Make a poster showing Jesus presiding over a feast or eucharist with bread and fish on the table. Make small fish badges which can be given to the congregation.

Devise a dance or a drama presentation about the despair of the fishermen, working all night without catching anything, the excitement of landing a huge catch and the happiness of sharing breakfast with Jesus. The dance or drama can be shared in the service after the gospel reading.

Adults

Invite members of the congregation to bring to the service something which speaks to them of fish or fishing. Anglers may choose to bring their rod and line; cooks may choose to bring a fish recipe. Others may choose to bring a picture, a poem or a text from Scripture. During the Peace invite them to display and discuss these items. Individuals with similar interests may group their contributions.

A range of ideas can be developed in discussion, teaching or preaching, including:

- our experiences of going fishing;
- our experiences of cooking fish;
- our experiences of sharing a fish meal;
- the central role of fishermen among the disciples;

- the symbol of the fish among early Christians;
- the disciples sharing a breakfast of fish with the Risen Jesus;
- shared meals in the life of the church today.

Teaching point

After his resurrection Jesus shared a meal of bread and fish with the disciples. Later the fish became an important symbol for the early Church. The Greek word for fish, ICHTHUS, makes up the initial letter for 'Jesus Christ, God's Son, Saviour'.

Repair Shop (4th Sunday after Easter)
Scripture: Read John 21:15–22

The Apostle Peter has a key place in the gospel narrative. He was among the first apostles to be called and was the first to proclaim recognition of Jesus as the Christ. At Jesus' trial, however, Peter's commitment had been tested and failed. Just as Jesus had predicted, Peter had denied Jesus three times before the cock crowed. Now, after the resurrection, Jesus offers Peter the chance of making a threefold affirmation of commitment in place of the threefold denial. Peter's personal restoration carried with it the responsibility to share Christ's pastoral concern for his followers.

Image

The narrative of Jesus' conversation with Peter highlights the way in which Jesus' resurrection brings forgiveness, healing and restoration. The meaning of Easter is that the resurrection of Jesus brings restoration to the fallen. We can begin to appreciate Peter's experience of restoration and the Bible's teaching about forgiveness by exploring our own experiences of having things repaired or repairing them ourselves.

Aims

The aims of this session are to:

- build on our experiences of mending and restoring things;
- understand the image of mending and restoring relationships;
- see the resurrection of Christ as bringing mending and restoration.

Children

Make a display of things which are broken, including for example: a clock which does not work; a toy which is obviously broken; a vase or plate which has fractured. Add to the display any pictures of people at work in the repair shop, including for example: the mechanic at work on a car; the cobbler mending a shoe. Talk about the children's experiences of things breaking and needing repair. Concentrate on the people who do the work of repair.

Draw out ideas of:

- the shoemaker reheeling shoes;
- the clockmaker repairing a clock;
- the mechanic repairing a car;
- parents repairing a toy;
- the electrician repairing the washing machine;
- the repairers at work in the teddy bear hospital.

Invite the children to make a display about the repair shop and about the people working there. For example, make a collection of broken toys and the tools needed to mend them. Make a collage of people who mend, using lots of things they need in the collage: a piece of clock for the clockmaker; an old piece of shoe leather for the shoemaker. Mend something that is broken or repair something that is torn and display the fruits of your work. Make a poster of tools needed in the repair shop.

Devise a dance or a drama presentation about the breakdown of a car, the gradual grinding to a stop, the frustration of being broken down, the arrival of the mechanic, and the feeling of restoration when the repair is completed. The dance or drama can be shared in the service after the gospel reading.

Adults

Invite members of the congregation to bring something to the service which is broken and needs the attention of the mender, for example a watch, a clock, or a torn garment. Others may prefer to bring some of the tools they use in mending things, for example a screwdriver or a needle and thread. During the Peace invite them to discuss what they have brought and to talk about how the broken things can be mended.

A range of ideas can be developed in discussion, teaching or preaching, including:

- our experiences of the car breaking down;
- our experiences of household appliances breaking down;
- our experiences of breaking things;
- our experiences of people who mend things;
- our own skills in mending;
- broken relationships and how they are mended;
- Peter's experience of restoration;
- our experience of the restoration which comes from Jesus' resurrection.

Teaching point

During Jesus' trial Peter had denied him three times. After the resurrection Jesus mends the broken relationship with Peter. The resurrection of Jesus offers healing and restoration to us as well.

Journeys (5th Sunday after Easter)

Scripture: Read Mark 16:1–8

On the Sunday before the Ascension, we return to the gospel account of the Easter event. On Easter Sunday, John's account was used; now it is Mark's account. Mark gives a clear account of a series of journeys. Mary Magdalene, Mary the mother of Jesus and Salome journeyed to the grave, entered the tomb, and found the tomb empty apart from the young man robed in white. He sent them out on another journey with a message for the disciples and Peter. The message was that Jesus was journeying ahead of them.

Image

The Christian life is often described as a journey. The invitation of Easter is to join that journey in the power of the resurrection. The resurrected Jesus both leads the way and travels as a companion on the path. This theme is clearly emphasized by Mark's succinct coverage of the events of Easter Sunday. We can begin to appreciate Mary's experience on that Easter Sunday morning by exploring our own experiences of journeys.

Aims

The aims of this session are to:

- build on our experiences of journeys;
- understand the journey as an image of the resurrected life;
- shape our response to the Easter journey.

Children

Make a display of different forms of travel. Include illustrations of people walking, riding bicycles and riding on horseback. Include cars, buses, trains, aeroplanes and ships. Try to find some toy cars, buses, trains, aeroplanes and ships. Collect some travel brochures. Find some road atlases or pin a large road map to the wall.

Draw out ideas of:

- different types of journeys;
- journeys the children have enjoyed;
- walking;
- travelling by train;
- travelling by ship;
- travelling by aeroplane;
- travelling by car;
- why people travel;
- journeys we would like to make.

Invite the children to make a display about journeys. Some may like to write about a journey they have undertaken. Some may like to bring toy cars or trains and arrange a layout of railways and roadways. Design a collage showing all different ways of travel and different places to be visited. Design a set of pictures telling the story of a journey from beginning to end. Show how travel has changed over the years.

Devise a dance or a drama presentation about the journey to the tomb on Easter Sunday, showing the apprehension, the discovery that the stone has been rolled away, the conversation with the young man robed in white and the journey away from the tomb to tell others.

Adults

Invite members of the congregation to bring to the service something which speaks to them about journeys. Some may choose to bring a map or postcards/photographs of places they have visited. Seasoned ramblers may choose to bring their walking stick, while motorcyclists may choose to bring their crash helmet. During the Peace invite them to undertake a journey round the church to discover and to talk about what others have brought.

A range of ideas can be developed in discussion, teaching or preaching, including:

- our experiences of journeys;
- journeys we have enjoyed;
- the feeling of discovery and progress when we find new places;
- the image of the journey in the Christian faith;
- the journey made by the women to the tomb;
- the journey to which Jesus calls us;
- Jesus' journey from Easter Sunday onwards to today.

Teaching point

The resurrection of Jesus was not the end of the story, but the beginning of something new. After the resurrection Jesus went on ahead of the disciples and challenged them to share in his journey.

Crowns (Sunday after Ascension Day)

Scripture: Read Luke 24:45–53

Each of the four gospels ends in a different way. The writer of Luke's Gospel is different from the other three gospel writers in that he set out to write a second book telling the continuing story of the early Church. The second book, the Acts of the Apostles, picks up the tale precisely where the first book, the Gospel of Luke, ends. It is the story of the ascension which so clearly links the two books. The gospel ends with the words, 'Jesus departed from them and was taken up into heaven.'

Image

The story of the ascension of Jesus can be very puzzling until the imagery is put into the context of the Old Testament from which it is derived. Especially in some of the Psalms of the Old Testament, ascension and going up is part of the imagery of the ceremony of coronation and king-making. The ascension of Christ affirms the Kingship of Christ. We can begin to experience the significance of the Bible's teaching about the Kingship of Christ by exploring our own images of kings and queens, and more especially of the crown as a symbol of kingship.

Aims

The aims of this session are to:

- build on our ideas about crowns;
- develop our understanding of the Kingship of Jesus;
- see the ascension as a proclamation of Jesus' Kingship.

Children

Make a display of stamps and coins which show the monarch's head wearing a crown. Ask the children what they notice in common about these coins and stamps. Look out pictures of royalty wearing crowns. Make a cardboard crown and wear it when the children arrive.

Draw out the ideas of:

- why coins and stamps carry the sovereign's head;
- why kings and queens wear crowns;
- what the crown symbolizes;
- the importance and authority of the sovereign;
- the honour and majesty of the sovereign;

- what kings and queens do;
- the Kingship of Jesus;
- he ascension as the story of enthronement.

Invite the children to make a display about crowns in the church. For example, collections of coins and stamps can be displayed. Draw large size pictures of coins. Design a postage stamp including the crowned monarch. Design a collage of a royal procession. Make a pattern by rubbing the surface of coins showing the royal head. Display a collection of products showing the royal crest. Make crowns for the children to wear, decorated with bright jewels.

Select music which evokes the pomp and dignity of a royal occasion and develop a stately dance or a drama presentation. Let each child wear a crown. The dance or drama can be shared in the service after the gospel reading.

Adults

Invite members of the congregation to bring something to the service which speaks to them of kings and queens, or more especially of coronations. Those who remember the most recent coronation may choose to bring a coronation mug or some other souvenir. Others may choose to bring a souvenir stamp or a picture of a royal procession. Others may like to make a crown. Display these symbols around the church and talk about them during the Peace.

A range of ideas can be developed in discussion, teaching or preaching, including:

- our images of kings and queens;
- media images of royalty;
- visits to see the crown jewels;
- the symbolic power of coronation;
- what is meant by calling Jesus King;
- the symbolism of the ascension as enthronement;
- the Ascension as the feast of Christ the King.

Teaching point

The story of the ascension speaks of Jesus being enthroned as King, in a way similar to the enthronement of the Jewish kings of old. The ascension theme is the feast of Christ the King.

Wind (Pentecost)

Scripture: Read Acts 2:1–11

Both in his gospel and in the Acts of the Apostles, Luke is much concerned with the activity of the Holy Spirit. The Holy Spirit is the guarantee of the presence of God among the people of God. In this passage Luke describes the coming of the Holy Spirit to the early Church on the day of Pentecost, after the period of waiting following the ascension. According to Luke's understanding, it is the presence of the Holy Spirit which constitutes the early Church as God's people and makes them the legitimate heirs to the old Israel where the Holy Spirit was active in earlier times. Right at the beginning of this narrative, the image is used of 'the rush of mighty wind'.

Image

One of the most powerful biblical images for the Spirit of God is that of the wind. The very close relationship between the idea of wind, breath and spirit is demonstrated by the fact that the same word is used for all three ideas, both in the Hebrew language of the Old Testament (*ruach*) and the Greek language of the New Testament (*pneuma*). We can begin to experience the significance of the Bible's teaching about God the Holy Spirit by exploring our own experiences of the wind.

Aims

The aims of the session are to:

- build on our ideas of the wind;
- develop our idea of wind as an image of the Holy Spirit;
- see Pentecost as the feast of the Holy Spirit.

Children

If it is a windy day, go outside to experience the wind. Feel the wind blow against your face. Feel the wind tug your kite into the sky. See the wind turn the sails of the windmill. See the wind blow washing inside out on the line. If it is not a windy day, set up an electric fan inside. Feel the breeze and see what it can do.

Draw out the ideas of:

- our experiences of a windy day;
- the sounds of the wind: whistling, banging, sweeping;
- the feel of the wind: caressing, soothing, pushing;
- the smell of the wind: spreading scents;
- the power of the wind: empowering sailing boats and windmills;
- the fascination of the wind;
- where the wind comes from and where the wind goes.

Invite the children to make a display about the wind in church. For example, make a large collage showing what it is like on a windy day, with sailing boats, kites and washing on the line. Make a weather vane. Make wind chimes and mobiles. Place them in a draught or near an electric fan. Make wind instruments and play them. Make hand windmills and model windmills. Go and fly a kite. Blow up balloons. Sail a model boat.

Imagine the wind is getting up and blowing through a forest. The wind shakes the branches of the trees. The wind picks up leaves from the forest floor, throws them into the air and drops them again. Express these ideas in dance or drama and share the dance or drama between the New Testament reading and the Gospel reading in the service.

Adults

Invite members of the congregation to bring something from home which speaks to them about the power of the wind. These may include things like a wind chime, a wind instrument, a weather vane, a model glider, a model sailing boat. Others may prefer to bring a picture about a windy day or a poem. Before the Scripture readings invite them to discuss what they have chosen and to display the objects in appropriate groupings.

A range of ideas can be developed in discussion, teaching or preaching, including:

- our experiences of a windy day;
- the different moods of the wind;
- the creative and the destructive face of the wind;
- the image of wind for the Holy Spirit;
- the experience of God as wind;
- the experience of the disciples on the Day of Pentecost;
- the experience of the spirit in the Church today.

Teaching point

The wind is a powerful image in which to speak of God the Holy Spirit. Luke speaks of the Holy Spirit coming to the disciples on the Day of Pentecost with sounds like a strong wind blowing.

APPENDIX A

ELAINE BARDWELL

PRUDENTIUS: HYMN FOR THE
LIGHTING OF THE EVENING LAMP

Aurelius Prudentius Clemens (AD 348–405) has been described as the greatest Christian Latin poet, often in the same breath as Horace, Vergil or Catullus. He was born, lived and worked in Spain, but is known to have visited Rome, the imperial capital. What little information we have about Prudentius is derived from his poetry, especially from the *Praefatio* ('Preface') which he wrote towards the end of his life to introduce his collected works. Having received the standard Roman education in literature and rhetoric, he became a lawyer and held public office at least twice. He was honoured in some way by the Emperor Theodosius, possibly with a position at court. Towards the end of his life he decided to concentrate on writing poetry in praise of God.

A thoroughly Roman patriot, he was nevertheless fully committed to the Christian faith as well. His work entitled *Liber Cathemerinon* ('Book for the Daily Round') is a series of Christian hymns written for the ordinary events of everyday life (e.g. rising, eating, lamplighting). These poems are rather long, which suggests that they were not intended for liturgical use in the way that Ambrose's hymns were. However, the fifth poem, *Inventor rutili*, found its way by the ninth century into the ceremonies of the Easter Vigil. In certain churches, especially in Germany, it was sung in procession after the kindling of the new fire at the beginning of the Paschal Liturgy. Yet in its original context it had been Prudentius' intention for this ode to be used at the lighting of the evening lamp, traditionally known as the *Lucernarium*. The greeting of newly-kindled light each evening, with a song of thanksgiving and praise to God, was already an ancient custom by the fourth century. It seems that when the ceremonies of fire and light at the Easter Vigil developed out of the *Lucernarium*, the strong imagery of the Crossing of the Red Sea in Prudentius' hymn made it a natural choice for use in this Easter context. Perhaps the poem was used for private devotion when it was first written and it might likewise commend itself to the devotions of Christians in the present day.

HYMN FOR THE LIGHTING OF THE EVENING LAMP

I

Good Lord,
Creator of the red-glowing light of evening,
who divides times and seasons in their due order,
as the sun dips down and dread darkness rushes on,
O Christ, restore light to your faithful ones.

Although you have adorned your realm with countless stars,
and the sky with the lamp of the moon,
yet, at the striking of flint,
you teach us to seek light from a stone-born spark,
that we might know our hope is firmly established on you, O Christ,
our steadfast rock and the source of our fire and light.

These little sparks we feed in lamps drenched in dripping oil
or upon dry torches,
and we mould rush candles,
coating them with the flower-scented wax of the combs
when the honey has been pressed from them.

The lively flame flourishes,
whether it is in a little earthenware hollow,
which supplies liquid fuel to an insatiable linen wick,
or pinewood brings its sustenance of pitch,
or warm tow drinks up the smooth wax.

Hot nectar drips from the molten top,
drop by drop in fragrant tears,
for the fiery flame causes a burning stream
to weep from the drenched summit.

And so, because of your gifts, Father,
our halls are resplendent indeed
and the light rivals the absent day
and makes night flee in defeat and despair.

II

And who could not discern the source of the swift light
emanating from God on high?
Like Moses who certainly saw God
as a flame of conspicuous light in the thorny bush.
Blessed was he who was deemed worthy
to see the ruler of the heavenly throne amidst the holy briars,
and was ordered to go unshod
and with bare feet to keep that holy place undefiled.

His people, those of glorious lineage,
weak but held safe by the merits of their ancestors,
accustomed to living under barbarian masters,
are now free and follow the divine fire
through the wilderness long and far.

As they make their way, pitching and striking camp,
in the middle of the dark night,
a ray, more sparkling than the sun,
leads the wakeful masses,
its splendour going on ahead of them.

III

But the King of the Nile's shores,
raging in his envy and hostility,
sends forth his mighty command
and orders his swift armies to go to war
and his iron-clad troops to sound the battle signal.

His men take up their weapons
and gird themselves with menacing swords
and the sombre war trumpet sounds its call.
This warrior trusts in his spears,
that one fastens flying arrow tips onto swift shafts.
The troops amass in infantry formations
whilst others mount their quick chariots
with their horses and flying wheels
and they spread forth their banners of war
famous for their swelling dragons.

Here, former bondage now left behind,
the race once burned up in the Egyptian heat,
at last rests, exhausted, in a strange land,
on the shores of the Red Sea.
But the grim enemy is at hand with their treacherous leader,
and with mighty strength launches into battle.

Moses firmly orders his people forward into the Sea,
to advance with brave and confident steps.
The waters rupture to make a way for the travellers,
creating an accessible path between the banks,
the flood standing upright in glassy walls on both sides
whilst the people pass by along the bed of the sea split asunder.

Now come the warriors, under their wicked king,
incited by bitter hatred and thirsting to shed Hebrew blood,
and they dare to trust themselves to that hollow in the sea.
The royal columns rush in headlong,
like a whirlwind through the midst of the flood,
but the mingling waters now roll back
flying back to meet up together once more.
Then see the shipwreck
of chariots and horses and weapons and princes and bodies
floating here and there,
a sorrowful end to the royal garrison.

Who could worthily sing your praises, O Christ?
You who conquered Pharaoh,
who, by your right hand, forced him after various afflictions,
to yield to you, the guardian of justice.
Who commands the sea, impassable in its raging tides,
to leap apart and provide a safe passage,
with you as guide to your people,
but bids that rapacious flood consume the ungodly.

IV

At your words the barren desert rocks
pour forth their gushing waters,
and new streams issue forth from the cleft flint,
giving drink to the people thirsting beneath the burning sky.

Water which lies like bitter poison in the ominous lake,
by virtue of wood becomes as sweet as honey.
And it is by wood that all that is bitter tastes more sweet,

for, human hope, when fixed to the Cross, grows strong.
Then the camp fills with food like snow,
dropping down more thickly than icy hail,
and with these delicacies the people produce a feast
which Christ bestows out of the starry sky.
And the wind with rainy breath,
conveys light-winged birds in a dense cloud,
who, once their formation is dispersed,
flow onto the ground and do not return to flight.

V

These rewards were once brought to our ancestors,
by the outstanding love of the one and only God
and it is by his assistance that we too eat,
feeding our hearts with mystic feasts.

He calls the exhausted across the straits of the world
leading his people and dividing the storms.
Those souls, thrown about by a thousand hardships,
he instructs to go to the native land of the righteous.
There all the ground is fragrant,
covered with red roses and rich marigolds,
with tender violets and fine crocuses,
watered by running rivulets.
And there too are balsam trees, sending out slender shoots
and rare cinnamon wafts its scent
and so too that leaf of pure nard borne from its hidden source
to the mouth of the River Ganges beside which it grows.

Blessed souls in the lush meadows
celebrate with pleasing harmony,
singing hymns with fine melodies
and treading upon the lilies with white feet.
And there also are the guilty spirits
who have their holiday from hell's punishments
on that night when the holy God returned
to the hopeful from the stagnant waters of Hades.
Not as the Morning Star, rising from Ocean at dawn,
stains the darkness with its flashing torch,
but here is one greater than the Sun,
to the earth in mourning at the Cross of her Lord,
he restores the new day.

Hell grows faint and its punishments diminish
and the people of the shadows rejoice,
freed from the fires, released from their prison,
and even the rivers of sulphur no longer burn in their customary fashion.

VI

We pass the night with holy joys,
in festal gatherings,
and we heap up fruitful prayers,
as we keep our watch
and offer our sacrifices in the shrines we have made.

The lamps are suspended on their swaying ropes,
and flicker against the roof panels above
and the lights are nurtured by the sluggish slopping oil,
as the flame throws out light through the transparent glass.
You might believe that the starry sky itself,
stood above us, adorned by the constellations,
where the Plough directs its team of oxen,
and everywhere the bright evening stars twinkle abroad.

O how noble a thing it is, Father,
which your flock offers you at this,
the beginning of the dewy night,
this light which is the most precious tribute,
this light by which we may see all your other gifts.
You are the true light to our eyes,
and the true light to our understanding.
You are a mirror within us and a mirror without.
Receive this light, which we offer in service,
dipped in the unction of peace-bearing oil,
through Christ, your only begotten Son,
almighty Father, in whom your glory is made visible,
who is our Lord and who is your only Son
and breathes the Paraclete from the Father's heart.
Through whom, splendour, honour, praise, wisdom,
majesty, goodness and your love,
extend your Kingdom of the threefold divinity
weaving together age to age for ever. Amen.

APPENDIX B

ELAINE BARDWELL

THE BLESSING OF THE EASTER CANDLE

The Gelasian Sacramentary bears the name of Gelasius (Pope from AD 492 to 496). He was associated with liturgical reform but the *Sacramentary* has little or nothing to do with him directly. The original version of this work can probably be dated to somewhere between 628 and 715. The earliest surviving manuscript is dated c. 750.

Sacramentaries grew out of the small *libelli* ('pamphlets') which certain early popes and others compiled containing special prayers for various celebrations of the eucharist. These were gathered over time into single books providing a variety of texts for different occasions. *The Gelasian Sacramentary* is thus a book for the presiding celebrant of the eucharist for most liturgies in the Church's year and was apparently compiled largely by presbyters in Rome. The Easter Vigil ceremony it contains began with the entrance of the clergy who stood before the altar to recite the *Agnus Dei*. Then the (arch)deacon presided over the lighting of the Paschal candle and sang the blessing, the *Deus mundi conditor*, over it including the blessing of the incense. When this was finished the presiding priest then stood up to recite the first of the prayers for the vigil itself.

The practice of the deacon singing the blessing over the Paschal candle was already established by the fourth century and may have originated in North Italy. It grew out of the practice of the *Lucernarium* which seems to have been held weekly on Saturday/Sunday evenings in many churches in which the lighting of the lamp was greeted with a hymn of thanksgiving and maybe also with incense. At the Easter Vigil, instead of a lamp, a candle was used as in its very composition it represented a microcosm of the whole creation. There were a number of compositions for blessing the Paschal candle which slowly developed into two traditions. One is the *Exultet/Preface*, familiar in the modern Holy Week liturgies and, in its present common form, is attributable to Ambrose. The other tradition is that of the *Deus, mundi conditor* as found here in *The Gelasian Sacramentary*.

THE GELASIAN SACRAMENTARY

O Lord, Creator of the world,
Author of the light, Maker of the stars,
Lord God, the world which was cast into darkness,
you have renewed with shining light.
God, through your almighty power,
the light has its beginning,
and so, calling upon you because of your works,
in this most holy vigil of the night,
and in prayer to your majesty
we make this offering of wax from among your gifts.
An offering which is undefiled by human sin,
not corrupted by any unholy anointing,
not infected by any profane fire,
but, made out of wax, oil and paper,
kindled in honour of your name,
we make this offering in allegiance and sacred devotion.

And so, it is worthy and right that this great mystery
and the wonderful sacrament of this night,
should be crowned with praises.
At that miracle of the Lord's resurrection,
the long established shades perceived
that day had been escorted in among them.
Even death, which once was condemned to everlasting night,
found the light of true splendour had been let in
and was astounded at being dragged along
as the captive in the Lord's triumphal procession.
And surprised too because when the first-created fell guilty
in his obstinate presumption, he had been condemned to slavery.
And so, rays of light now shine forth
in the marvellous magnificence of this night.
Therefore to revere this festival with true fervour of spirit,
in humility and with as much human devotion
as we can muster,
for you, our God, we set forth lights,
splendid and pleasing with their flames,
that as these are offered up with pure faith
so your creatures' commendations might be raised up too.

For it was by means of a light of flame, so it is said,
that the power of the Deity deigned to appear to Moses,

which shone forth and led the people out of a land of slavery
by going ahead with saving light.
It was the same light which came to the three young men,
set down in the fiery furnace by the tyrant's judgement,
and preserved their lives for gentler blandishments.

And, as the terror of the shadows is shut out
by the preceding grace of this light,
so too, Lord, by the dawning sovereignty of your majesty,
are the burdens of sin put away.
When, therefore, we marvel at the created thing,
we must also praise the creator.

Consider the bees, who are indeed thrifty in expenditure,
and most chaste in procreation.
They build little cells from flowing wax,
whose foundations the most masterly skill of human artifice
cannot match.
They gather flowers with their feet and do not harm the blooms.
They do not give birth to offspring, but bearing by mouth their brood,
the swarms return and provide a marvellous example
of the way in which Christ proceeded from the Father's mouth.
This virginal birth is fruitful and the Lord too clearly
thought this worthy to be followed and took his mother of flesh
together with virgin love.
Therefore, worthy Lord, such are the gifts offered at your holy altars,
to bring joy at the knowledge that the Christian faith
is firmly founded.

The Blessing over the Incense

And so, almighty God, pour out your generous blessing
upon this incense, and,
Invisible Ruler of all, increase the magnificence of this night,
that not only the sacrifice offered this night may be acceptable,
reflecting the mystery of your light,
but also, that this place may be sanctified by our celebrations,
driving out the wicked deceptions of the devil
and filling it with the goodness of your majesty.

Through our Lord Jesus Christ, your Son,
who lives with you and reigns in the unity of the Holy Spirit,
one God throughout all ages. Amen.